Four Seminars

Studies in Continental Thought

Martin Heidegger

Four Seminars

Le Thor 1966, 1968, 1969, Zähringen 1973

Translated by

Andrew Mitchell and François Raffoul

INDIANA
University Press
Bloomington & Indianapolis

This book is a publication of

Indiana University Press
601 North Morton Street
Bloomington, Indiana 47404-3797 USA

iupress.indiana.edu

Telephone orders 800-842-6796
Fax orders 812-855-7931

First published in German as
Vier Seminare. Le Thor 1966, 1968, 1969 – Zähringen 1973,
edited by Curd Ochwadt.
Frankfurt am Main: Vittorio Klostermann, 1977.

Also published in German in Martin Heidegger,
Gesamtausgabe, volume 15: *Seminare.*

First paperback edition 2012
© 1986 by Vittorio Klostermann, Frankfurt am Main
© 2003 by Indiana University Press

⊖ The paper used in this publication meets the minimum requirements
of the American National Standard for Information Science–Permanence
of Paper for Printed Library Materials, ANSI Z39.48-1992.

Manufactured in the United States of America

The Library of Congress catalogued the original edition as follows:

Heidegger, Martin, 1889–1976.
[Vier Seminare. English]
Four Seminars / Martin Heidegger; translated by
Andrew Mitchell and François Raffoul.
p. cm. – (Studies in Continental thought)
ISBN 0-253-34363-1 (cloth : alk. paper)
1. Philosophy. I. Title. II. Series.
B3279.H48V5413 2003
193–dc21
2003005390

ISBN 978-0-253-34363-5 (cl.)
ISBN 978-0-253-00881-7 (pbk.)
ISBN 978-0-253-00895-4 (electronic book)

2 3 4 5 6   17 16 15 14 13 12

Contents

Translators' Foreword   vii

Seminar in Le Thor 1966   1

Seminar in Le Thor 1968   10

Seminar in Le Thor 1969   35

Seminar in Zähringen 1973   64

German Translator's Afterword to *Vier Seminare*   85

Martin Heidegger, "The Provenance of Thinking"   93

Martin Heidegger, "Parmenides: Ἀληθείης εὐκυκλέος ἀτρεμὲς ἦτορ"   94

German Editor's Afterword to *Collected Edition*, volume 15   98

Endnotes to the Translation   101

Glossaries   113

   German–English   113

   English–German   116

Translators' Foreword

I. Situations

The *Four Seminars* of 1966, 1968, 1969, and 1973 grant us insight into Heidegger's thinking at the end of his career and towards the end of his life. In many regards they are the culmination of his work and the last intensive philosophical engagements of his life. These seminars present us with a Heidegger who has left fundamental ontology far behind, who has traversed the expanse of *Seynsgeschichtliche Denken*, be-ing-historical thinking, who has thought with the Greeks and has attempted to do so in a way that is "more Greek than the Greeks" (see below, 39), a Heidegger who has likewise struggled long and hard with the twin mountains of Nietzsche and Hölderlin, and the relation between them, a Heidegger on the way to language and still thinking the question concerning technology; in short, the *Four Seminars* present us with Heidegger at full stride towards the end of his long path. The circumstances surrounding these seminars are treated at length in the German translator's afterword following the text,[1] but a few opening remarks are in order.

At the end of his life-work, Heidegger remains what he was at its beginning, a German thinker, viewing himself in intimate relation to a long line of German thinkers from the history of philosophy, Kant, Hegel, Nietzsche, and Husserl to name only the brightest stars in the constellation. For this reason, these late engagements with France and French thought are all the more appealing to our intellectual circumspection. Here the thinker of the German homeland, German poetry, and German word origins, has placed himself on the foreign soil of France—foreign, to be sure, but nonetheless a "neighbor-people."[2] It is no accident that the first topic addressed in these seminars, in the 1966 Le Thor seminar, is that of Heraclitus' ξυνόν and the belonging-together of contraries. Throughout the seminars one is surprised to find a Heidegger who is continually reaching out to his French audience, citing texts like Descartes' *Discourse* or Husserl's *Cartesian Meditations* by their French titles, engaging in conversation with the poet René Char, passing references to French poets and painters like Mallarmé and Braque, not to mention Cézanne, drawing examples from the landscape around him, and considering the place of the French language for a thinking of being and its givenness. Yet this francophile Heidegger is certainly not the only Heidegger present.

To be sure, Heidegger does not cite Descartes in any laudatory fashion. Descartes remains, as he was in the 1937 *"Wege zur Aussprache,"* another name for the mathematical conception of nature and the philosophy of representational subjectivism. And when Heidegger treats of the French language, it is to say that *"il y a,"* as a translation of the German *"es gibt,"* is still "too ontic." A further complication in Heidegger's regard for France arises when we consider a post card that he wrote in the midst of the seminars (September 10, 1966) to Imma von Bodmershof.[3] The face of the postcard shows the church of Notre-Dame du Lac in Le Thor (Vaucluse); its back reads:

> Dear and respected friend,
> From a beautiful residence in Provence, in the vicinity of Petrarch and Cézanne, where Greece still speaks, I greet you heartily.
>
> > Yours,
> > Martin Heidegger

The French landscape is admirable not for its own merits, one could say, but for its transmission of the Greek voice. Indeed, in seeming confirmation of this, a poem Heidegger wrote for René Char concludes by asking whether Provence is not the bridge between Parmenides and Hölderlin.[4] And yet, would this not precisely mean that France and what is French surely do maintain a connection with the Greek? That if Greece can speak in France and if Greek is the language of philosophy, then French too could be a philosophical language? Certainly today there is no question as to the answer to this question, but is it not Heidegger who is held to maintain that philosophy can only speak in German or Greek? These *Four Seminars* open the possibility for a different view of the Heidegger-France relation.[5] As such, they constitute a crucial document for a Heideggerian understanding of homeland and national identity—they not only develop central ideas for such a thought, *they enact that thought itself.*

As to the texts, a few words should here be said. The single volume German edition of *Vier Seminare* is a German translation of the French seminar protocols gathered together into the French volume of Heidegger's writings, *Questions IV.*[6] These seminar protocols were read in Heidegger's presence at the time of composition. Curd Ochwadt's German translation, for its part, includes some further alterations of his own (most noticeably around the explanation of German words and phrases in the French texts), and appeared shortly after Heidegger's death. Heidegger nevertheless "monitored" this translation[7] and—as further testimony to the importance of these seminars for him—likewise "purposed" its adoption into the *Collected Edition* of his works.[8] It is this German text that is rendered into English in the following pages, though always with an eye to whatever light the French "original" may provide.

When the *Four Seminars* finally were published within Heidegger's *Collected Edition* (in the 1986 volume *Seminare,* GA 15) the German editor

Curd Ochwadt provided a further element for appreciating Heidegger's work in seminar: the manuscript of the text Heidegger presented in the concluding session of the 1973 Zähringen seminar, entitled "Parmenides: Ἀληθείης εὐκυκλέος ἀτρεμὲς ἦτορ." Heidegger later appended a brief preface to this piece, "The Provenance of Thinking," and both of these texts are supplied as appendices below. The former is the only manuscript from Heidegger's hand that we have from these seminars (indeed from any of the seminars published during Heidegger's lifetime), and thus a key document for illuminating Heidegger's seminar work method. It is worth comparing this text with the protocol from that last session for an insight into the functioning of the group and the process of transcription. By no means can we say that the seminar protocol "bastardize" the pristine thought of the singly composed text. Quite to the contrary, they develop it, comment upon it, and take it in various invigorating directions. Heidegger in conversation is no less a thinker than Heidegger at the *Schreibtisch*. Indeed, the seminar situation and enchanting locale present us with a Heidegger at ease and in command, following out tangents of thought with rapid development and returning back to the main line of his argument with unhurried facility. For a thinker who places so high a value upon "conversation" (*Gespräch*), it would certainly be startling if the situation were otherwise. It is our belief that the texts of these four seminars are of genuine value on a par with the works of Heidegger's own sole composition.

II. Topoi

The topical importance of these seminars cannot be reduced to a mere listing of themes. Every theme addressed is handled with an expert lucidity and seasoned appreciation for the subtleties of the matter at stake (*Sache*). This alone is enough to render the seminars "important" for Heidegger scholarship. Instead, the importance of these seminars is best appreciated by considering the new *topos* from which they speak. What follows are a few attempts to sketch the contours of that place:

ES GIBT AND LETTING

A major development in these seminars concerns Heidegger's rethinking and treatment of the "*es gibt*." Beginning from a reflection on the sense of *Ereignis* as event of the givenness of presence (described as the "event [*Ereignis*] of being as condition for the arrival of beings: being lets beings presence," see below, 59), Heidegger is then led to rethink the meaning of being as "letting." It is a matter, he states firmly, "of understanding that the deepest meaning of being is *letting* [*Lassen*]" (*ibid.*). Being is not the horizon for the encountering of beings, nor the "there is" of beings, and not simply time itself. Rather, being means now: Letting the being be (*Das Seiende sein-lassen*). What matters most is that this "letting" not be understood ontically, for that would mean that the philosophical opening sought here would close at once. This means: letting is not a cause, for causality still draws from the logic of beings and their "sufficient" grounding. Causality aims at the foundation of beings. To that extent, causality is foreign to what is proper to being (understood from "letting"). We should note that a few lines prior, Heidegger had already rejected causality as an inappropriate access to being: One can name being an origin, he says, "assuming that all ontic-causal overtones are excluded" (*ibid.*).

A second inappropriate motif when thinking the original meaning of "letting" is the reference to a "doing," if that supposes some activity of being, drawing from the philosophy of an acting subject. Letting is to be thought instead from "giving": hence Heidegger focuses on the expression "*es gibt*," and engages it further than in previous texts, including *Time and Being*. The expression "*es gibt*" should also be carefully distinguished from any ontic connotations, which the expressions "there is," or, in French, "*il y a*," still convey. The giving here in question should not refer primarily to a present being, or even to the *presence* of beings. The key is that the notion of giving is here approached independently from metaphysical beinghood, perhaps a remark intended at possible misunderstandings of the analyses found in *Time and Being*. Heidegger demonstrates this in several stages: First, if "it is tempting to understand '*Es gibt*' as meaning 'It lets [something] come to presence,'" (*ibid.*), this emphasis makes one conceive of the giving in "*es gibt*" ontically, i.e., in reference to a being. Secondly, the "giving" should be separated from presence itself, for the issue instead is to give thought to the "*es gibt*," to giving, from an interpretation of the "letting itself."

The "*es gibt*" is then understood in terms of the letting as such: "Presence is no longer emphasized, but rather the *letting* itself. '*Es gibt*' then has the precise meaning: '*to let* the presencing'" (*ibid.*). Pursuing further, Heidegger stresses here that the letting as such points not to the presence given, but to the gift of a giving as such, a giving which withdraws in the very movement of its event. One should therefore not say: "Being is," and neither: "There is being." Instead, one should say: it lets being (*Es läßt Sein*). One is then led to wonder whether the very name "being" is the most appropriate term to name the event of giving. In fact, Heidegger writes strikingly that "If the emphasis is: *to let* presencing, there is no longer room for the very name of being" (*ibid.*).

Heidegger in the end distinguishes three ways of understanding the "*es gibt*" and letting:

a) First, in reference to what is, to beings.

b) Second, when "the attention is drawn less towards *what* is given . . . than towards *the presencing* itself" (see below, 59–60).

c) Finally, when the emphasis is placed on the letting itself. With this last sense, one is engaging the question of *Ereignis*.

ENOWNING

A key remark is first made concerning the translation of the term. It is from the outset stated that the French translation of *Ereignis* by *avènement*, that is, "event" or "advent," and which corresponds to the ordinary usage of the term *Ereignis* in German, is unacceptable. Much more adequate is another rendering one finds in the French translation of *Time and Being*, namely *appropriement*, that is, "appropriation," or better: "enowning." Heidegger makes the important suggestion that being is to be thought from enowning, that in fact "Being is enowned through *enowning*" (see below, 60). A few lines further, one also reads: "Enowning enowns being [*das Ereignis ereignet das Sein*]."

One of the most important contributions of these seminars is the way in which Heidegger distinguishes between enowning and being, showing how enowning exceeds being and its economy. One should not think enowning with the help of the concepts of being or of the history of being, we are told. Enowning exceeds the ontological horizon, as it exceeds the Greek "sending" in the history of being. It then also appears that Heidegger's thought as such is not contained within the horizon of ontology, nor of the thought of being; he in fact explains that his thinking of the ontological difference—especially in the period from 1927 to 1936, which is taken to be the crux of this work—was a "necessary impasse" (*Holzweg*) (see below, 61). With respect to enowning's relation to the history of being, and to the epochs of being, a further crucial remark is made: There is no destinal epoch of *enowning*. Enowning is *not* an epoch of being, and nor is it the end of the history of being, in the sense in which the history of being would have "reached its end." Instead, one should say that from enowning, and insofar as it exceeds it, the history of being is able to appear *as* history of being. Further, the historical sendings of being are to be thought *from* Enowning. As Heidegger says strikingly: "Sending is from enowning [*Das Schicken ist aus dem Ereignen*]" (*ibid.*).

TECHNOLOGY

In the *Four Seminars*, Heidegger's thinking of technology culminates in a logic of replaceability (*Ersetzbarkeit*) and consumption (*Verbrauch*). "Being is being-replaceable" he writes, and in so doing names the countenance of being for our time (see below, 62). In a discussion that calls to mind Baudrillard sooner than it does Marx (the impetus for these reflections), Heidegger considers how the artificial "increasingly replaces 'natural' material," so much so that it is now essential for all these beings of consumption that they *"be already* consumed" (*ibid.*). This emphasis upon replacement and consumption distinguishes the era of technology from that of modern science. It is a new destiny of being to which Heidegger is responding and it is precisely in this response that Heidegger articulates the relation between positionality and enowning.

In these pages we find an explicit elucidation of the technological "veiling" of enowning, from illustrative images (positionality is the "photographic negative" of enowning; see below, 60) to necessary consequences (a *"finitude of being* must accordingly be assumed"; see below, 63). Positionality represents the completion of the logic governing metaphysics and *to that extent* it is likewise an opening. This "event" of an opening in completion, this reciprocal "need" of positionality and its other, this very "appropriation" which joins together the totalizing drive of technology to the thinking that would exceed it – all of this Heidegger painstakingly designates with the term *Ereignis* ("enowning"). Technological positionality, far from being seen negatively, is therefore the preparation or the announcement of enowning: "It means that thinking begins anew, so that in the essence of technology it catches sight of the heralding portent, the covering pre-appearance, the concealing pre-appearing of enowning itself" (see below, 61).

We should be careful not to think enowning anywhere outside this "heralding portent" or "concealing pre-appearing." Heidegger gives much thought to the co-belonging of positionality and enowning. In a sense, every one of the *Four Seminars* is concerned with such co-belonging as it informs technology: in 1966, Heraclitus' ξυνόν names the sharing and belonging together of contraries; in 1968, this difference within identity is thought in terms of a tear, and examined through Hegel's image of a "torn sock"; in 1969, it is cast in the explicit terms of positionality and enowning; finally, in 1973, it is addressed in a return to Parmenides where presence itself presences as τὸ ἐόν. In this way, the *Four Seminars* conduct the reader along Heidegger's transfigurative path: from technology through enowning, and on to a confrontation with the Greeks. And this even though "With enowning, it is no longer an issue of Greek thought" and philosophy is "no Greek way of ek-sisting, but rather a *hyper-Greek* way" (see below, 61, 38). It is a matter here, in the midst of technological replaceability, of bringing our ownmost into an open confrontation with Greek fate.

EXCESS

Technology can thus never completely veil enowning, or rather, the veiling of enowning is the event of enowning. Heidegger has previously thought this in terms of a "withdrawal" or "refusal" of being, as he does, for example, in the *Contributions to Philosophy (from Enowning).*[9] In these pieces, dating from 1936–1938, Heidegger considers the withdrawal of being as an abandonment that leaves the world a workshop of machination. The traces of that refusal, however, are still to be found (there are hints, he says then). Thirty years later, these ideas are reformulated in terms of "excess" (*Übermaß*). There is an excess to positionality, to machination, that the technological endeavor cannot program away or incorporate into its "economic standing-reserves" (see below, 62). It is excess which drives that technological endeavor, and excess to which the poet and thinker are exposed. In these seminars, this extra-economic moment of excess is now spoken of in terms of "indications" or the "heralding portent" (see below, 79, 61). Such a movement from withdrawal to excess informs the entirety of the discussion of enowning and positionality. Philosophy is always in relation to excess, "the dimension of the entirely excessive is that in which philosophy arises" (see below, 38). In remarking this excess, in attending to it, philosophy is likewise a response to positionality, and in this responding philosophy itself remains *in excess:* "Philosophy is indeed the answer of a humanity that has been struck by the excess of presence–an answer which is itself excessive" (*ibid.*).

III. Figures

The *Four Seminars* also provide lengthy considerations of various figures from the history of philosophy, considerations which shed valuable light on Heidegger's reading of the tradition (there are even rare references here to Wittgenstein and Marcuse). Five of the central figures to be mentioned are familiar to readers of Heidegger's work–Parmenides, Heraclitus, Kant, Hegel, and Husserl–Heidegger had already devoted considerable attention to each of these in previous lectures and published texts. One figure, however, is less common in the Heideggerian corpus, namely, Karl Marx. Apart from a short passage in the *Humanismusbrief*, it is within the pages of these *Seminars* that one finds Heidegger's most developed Marx interpretations. Marx is mentioned in *every one* of these seminars, but he receives the fullest treatment in 1969 and 1973.

Because of Marx's critique of consciousness it is often said (this was Marcuse's position) that there is a close proximity between Heidegger and Marx. However, Heidegger points to the metaphysical character of Marx's thought. Stressing that he does not read Marx in a political way, but metaphysically, Heidegger interprets Marxist thought in its fundamental situation within the history of being. More precisely, Heidegger stresses that Marx understands being from the notion of *production,* and man as the self-production of itself. However, "This practical concept of production can only exist on the basis of a conception of being stemming from metaphysics" (see below, 52). Heidegger identifies further that position, in the 1973 seminar, as the "thought of today" (perhaps an ironic passing reference to Sartre's famous statement, according to which Marxism is the unsurpassable philosophy of our times), that is, the nihilistic imperative of progress as imperative of ever new needs in which everything is replaceable in the perspective of an exploitation of everything that is (see below, 73). Positionality then proves to be the horizon and the truth of Marxist thought.

Turning to the other figures mentioned above, Heidegger's treatment of Parmenides in these pages focuses upon his understanding of being as presence. Parmenides' claim that being *is* leads Heidegger to explore the idea of presence itself presencing. For Heidegger, Being "is" means "presence presences," or rather, as he will have it, there is a presencing of presencing itself. These reflections upon the presencing of presencing lead Heidegger to speak of the "inapparent" (see below, 79): The presencing which presences presences inapparently. Consequently, these readings of Parmenides are also important for the link they forge between Parmenides and Heidegger's own thinking of a phenomenology of the inapparent.

In regard to Heraclitus, two aspects of Heidegger's reading are to be emphasized. First, months before the Fink seminar, the focus of these sessions is upon the relation between contraries in Heraclitus' thought. Heidegger approaches this question by attending to Heraclitus' thinking of the ξυνόν in the fragments. The presentation is dense and thoughtful and carried out in explicit antagonism to the Hegelian dialectic. Second, there is a presence of poetry throughout these sessions of the 1966 seminar. Each session opens with an epigram from René Char, who himself participates in the sessions as well. The sessions close with Char and Heidegger discussing Heraclitus' proximity to poetry. This situation is not an arbitrary one given the topic of the seminar, belonging-together. As such, the reading of Heraclitus here performed enriches our understanding of the thinker-poet relation in Heidegger's work.

Heidegger's interpretation of Kant in the *Four Seminars* is noteworthy in three regards: first, Kant, who is supposedly the most systematic of systematic philosophers, is shown to actually reveal the impossibility of the system and the abyssal character of reason. The ground of a system can only remain an "idea" for Kant, which suggests that reason is unable to provide its ultimate grounding. Heidegger cites a passage from the *Critique of Pure Reason* where Kant explains that "Unconditioned necessity, which we so indispensably require as the last bearer of all things, is for human reason the veritable *abyss* " (see below, 17). The abyss thus exposed is indicative of reason's finitude and "powerlessness." Second, Kant's thought is strongly contrasted against the Greek world: "For the Greeks, things appear. For Kant, things appear to me," Heidegger states in 1969 (see below, 36). Kant understands being in terms of the objectivity of nature, an objectivity experienced in mathematical-scientific terms. Third, this does not mean that Kant's thinking and categories are "abstract." Heidegger notes this and refers to the schematism of the first *Critique,* where he strikingly remarks that the schematism is "the Kantian way of discussing being and time" (see below, 69). Returning to Kant in the *Four Seminars*, Heidegger extends the interpretation of Kant begun during the Marburg period of the twenties.

As to Hegel, here we find the only substantial treatment in the Heideggerian oeuvre of Hegel's foundational *Differenzschrift*, in the 1968 seminar in Le Thor. Heidegger's *line-by-line* analysis of this text focuses upon the nature of separation, division, and difference within Hegelian thought as well as with the reconciliation of these in absolute non-dichotomy. The German editor's afterward to the *Collected Works* volume provides interesting factual detail on Heidegger's apparent misquotation of Hegel in the central image of the seminar, his claim that "a torn sock is better than a mended one" (see below, 11). Along with a careful unpacking of the term *"Aufhebung,"* the 1968 seminar also devotes explicit attention to the ideas of reflection, production, and contraction in Hegel's work. Hegel is likewise dealt with in the course of the 1966 seminar on Heraclitus. In 1966 the Hegelian notion of dialectic is criticized in favor of Heraclitus' thinking of co-belonging. In 1968, the Hegelian thought of co-belonging is itself more fully articulated and it is a valuable exercise to compare the two.

Lastly, in the 1973 Zähringen seminar, Heidegger returns to Husserl and the problem of categorical intuition, and does so nearly fifty years after his first consideration of this material in the 1925 lecture course, *History of the Concept of Time: Prolegomena.*[10] Yet, whereas in the 1925 course, Heidegger was very critical of Husserl's phenomenology, even going so far as to deem it "unphenomenological" (!), here he stresses through minute and detailed analyses that Husserl's discovery of categorial intuition is itself already a discovery of being: "Husserl touches upon or struggles with the question of being in chapter six of the sixth *Logical Investigation,* with the notion of 'categorial intuition.'" (see below, 65). Some critical remarks are also made concerning the relation between Dasein and consciousness. Beginning by stating firmly that, "In the entirety of modern thought, stemming from Descartes, subjectivity thus constitutes the barrier to the unfolding of the question of being" (see below, 70), Heidegger takes issue with Husserl's philosophy of consciousness and intentionality. For, the "addition" of intentionality to consciousness does not solve the problem of a subjectivity self-enclosed in its *cogitationes:* "Husserl remains trapped in immanence" (*ibid.*); consequently, "with Husserl, the sphere of consciousness is not challenged, much less shattered" (*ibid.*) . . . In contrast to Husserl, Heidegger insists that one needs to start from *outside* of the *ego cogito,* which is precisely what the term Dasein seeks to indicate.

Before closing, one further figure from the history of philosophy should be mentioned here, and that is Martin Heidegger himself. Throughout these seminars Heidegger's own work receives careful scrutiny and, often, correction. This is nowhere more apparent than in the case of *Being and Time*. To list only a few of the numerous criticisms to be encountered here: the book's central term "Dasein" was formulated "very awkwardly and in an unhelpful way," Heidegger says; the very language of *Being and Time* "lacks assurance"; and, perhaps most strikingly, the book itself lacks "a genuine knowledge of the history of being" (see below, 69, 78, 51). Each of these remarks is valuable for understanding Heidegger's relation to Heidegger as a figure within the history of philosophy. Beyond these criticisms, however, of even greater worth are Heidegger's own ruminations upon his path of thought, from the early focus upon the "meaning of being" all the way to his late conception of a "topology of being." He likewise provides precious clues for understanding his later thought and its debt to phenomenology, going so far as to describe his own "tautological thinking" as the "primordial sense of phenomenology" (see below, 80). This leads him to name the current state of his thinking a "phenomenology of the inapparent" (*ibid.*), a name that both recalls the methodology that provided Heidegger with the essential impetus of his career, while bringing that methodology to its most extreme possibility and formulation.

* * *

It is our hope that in presenting these valuable texts to an English speaking audience, the thought of Martin Heidegger will be carried a little further and in new directions, not only within the narrow confines of "Heideggerianism." The vibrant character and adventurous quality of Heidegger's thinking in the concluding years of his life is an invitation for such tasks. In many respects, the *Four Seminars* present Heidegger's last word on a variety of philosophical topics, it is only fitting that he should have the last word here. Returning in a January 1973 letter to René Char—after the death of their host in Le Thor, Mme. Marcelle Mathieu—to the situations, topoi, and figures of the *Four Seminars*, Heidegger writes:

> For days now, a small picture of the Lagnes village has stood before me. Or else it lay upon the work desk among the other pictures showing Les Busclats and Le Thor, ready for a moment of recollection upon the days spent in the beloved Provence. Lagnes, the birth place of Marcelle Mathieu, between the Rebanqué heights and the valleys of Les Grands Camphoux, from where death has now taken her away. The circle of the named places itself belongs to a region; its center is formed by Les Busclats, and is directed in the west towards Le Thor. This region, in turn, finds its own distinct borders at Mont Ventoux and at the Montagne Sainte-Victoire with Bibemus.
>
> A mere listing of places? So it seems. But what is proper to a place is contained in the way that each gathers, casts, and attunes the people dwelling there in their deeds and allowances, their poetizing and thinking.[11]

We would like to thank John Sallis for his initial and continual support of this project. We are grateful to Ryan Hellmers for his careful and detailed reading of the entire manuscript, and to James Ryan for his numerous suggestions and clarifications. The work is much improved due to their efforts. We are also grateful to Amy Alexander for her improvements of numerous sentences during the course of the translating. On the German side, we would like to thank Dr. Peter Trawny for his expertise in explaining the finer points of Heidegger's German, and Prof. Dr. Heinrich Hüni for his careful discrimination between editions of the text. Finally, we would like to thank Janet Rabinowitch and Dee Mortensen of Indiana University Press for their patience in this venture.

Chamonix Mont-Blanc, July 2002

Four Seminars

À M. H.
[Martin Heidegger]

L'automne va plus vite en avant, en arrière que
le râteau du jardinier. L'automne ne se précipite pas
sur le cœur qui exige la branche avec son ombre.

Les Busclats 11 sept. 1966
René Char[12]

The seminar from 1966 (eight years after the lecture in Aix-en-Provence: "Hegel and the Greeks") consists of seven conversations. The first two concerned Parmenides and the following five were all in regard to Heraclitus. Two young Italian friends, Ginevra Bompiani and Giorgio Agamben, joined Vezin, Fédier, and Beaufret. At that time, no protocols were kept. From the combined notes of the participants, however, a report can be given of three of the Heraclitus conversations. These took place on September 5th, in a garden of Le Thor; on the 9th, in Le Rebanqué; and on the 10th, in Les Busclats.

September 5

> "Upon its poetic cliffs, Le Thor rose up.
> Mont Ventoux, the mirror of the eagles
> towered into view."[13]

After two conversations on Parmenides' poem, we searched for a guiding thread for the reading of Heraclitus' fragments. The decisive question here is: to which words of Heraclitus should the elucidation direct itself? We certainly have many words before us: *logos, physis,* world, strife, fire, the singular-one, etc. Taking our cue from a comment provided by Aristotle,[14] we could follow the tradition and take Fragment 1 of the Diels-Kranz edition as the beginning of Heraclitus' writing.[15] According to Diogenes Laertius, Heraclitus is supposed to have laid them in the temple of Artemis in Ephesus for their safekeeping. The other fragments are arranged by Diels-Kranz according to the alphabetical order of the authors who have cited them—from Aetius to Theophrastus—except for fragment 2, which was handed down by Sextus Empiricus and almost directly linked by him to fragment 1: "When before going further he adds . . ."

We will therefore take as our guiding thread the logos, a concern right from the start of fragment 1:

τοῦ δὲ λόγου τοῦδ' ἐόντος ἀεὶ ἀξύνετοι γίνονται ἄνθρωποι . . .

Right away we encounter a first difficulty.

Already in antiquity, Aristotle had observed (same reference as above) that the word ἀεὶ can refer just as much to what precedes it as to what follows it. Is it indeed λόγος that is named the ἐὼν ἀεὶ? Or is it said of the humans, that they *never cease* to remain in ignorance of it? Against Burnet and Diels, though with Kranz, Heidegger gives preference to the relation of ἀεὶ with what follows it. His reason for this decision is not that of Kranz, namely that the word is followed by adverbs (καὶ πρόσθεν . . . καὶ τὸ πρῶτον) which would determine the sense of ἀεί. The basis for Heidegger's decision is that he does not read ἐόντος as an epithet of λόγου, but instead, literally, as the genitive of ἐόν: the being in its being. In his more paratactical than syntactical reading, τοῦ δὲ λόγου τοῦ δ'ἐόντος are taken as *corresponding precisely to one another*, which also determines the separation of the fourth word in the sentence: τοῦδε into τοῦ δέ.

We thus do not read:

Now of λόγος, as what is everlastingly (ἀεί) true, humans are without understanding;

and also not:

Now of λόγος, of that which is true, the humans are ever (ἀεί) without any understanding;

but rather:

Now of λόγος, *of beings in their being, the humans never have an understanding.*

What is said here would thus be the sameness of λόγος and ἐόν, in the sense in which Parmenides likewise says in his poem:

"For it is indeed the same, both thinking and being."

It is at least from this reading that we are to understand what Heidegger said in *The Principle of Reason* from 1956, namely that "a belonging to being . . . speaks in all that is said in the Greek word λόγος," in other words that, "λόγος names being," or that, "Though it had other names in early Western thinking, 'being' means λόγος."[16]

We will now read fragment 1 as a whole:

"But of λόγος, of the beings in their being, humans remain constantly outside of all understanding, as much before they have heard as after they have first heard; for while everything occurs according to the λόγος of which I speak, they are indeed like the inexperienced, when they attempt such words and works as I set forth, in that I distinguish each thing according to its essence and I say it as it is. But what the other humans do while awake escapes from them just as what was present [*gegenwärtig*] to them while asleep again conceals itself from them."

Fragment 1, which makes λόγος into the foremost fundamental word of all the fundamental words, is supported in this by fragment 72, as reported by Marcus Aurelius:

"With what they most belong together. . . , from this they diverge, and hence: all that they encounter everyday appears to them in a foreign light [ξένα φαίνεται]."

The text apparently contains a paradox. Aren't the things that one comes across everyday entirely familiar? To just what an extent are they supposed to show themselves in a foreign light? In so far as the humans, when they diverge [*entzweien*] from the λόγος, only see a side of what they encounter; to the same extent, the thing encountered is, as it were, estranged from itself.

The fragment thus names the humans, insofar as they depart from being, in order to then fall from being and upon beings. This is seen in *Being and Time,* where *"departure from being"* is made to designate such a fall or falling away (upon beings).[17] What Heraclitus says, however, is in no way related to the Fall of Man, but belongs to the Difference between being and beings itself, by which the humans are even more originally gathered. The interpretation of fallenness as the Fall of Man, on the contrary, is itself the setting aside of this difference. Since here the difference between being and beings is maintained, even Platonism with its denigration of what would be mere appearance remains yet to come. The ξένα of Heraclitus are not *any less beings,* but rather are themselves beings of such a sort that they show themselves as *foreign* to those who depart from the difference. Heraclitus is not yet as *antagonistically* disposed toward the *foreign* as Plato is.[18]

If we now turn back from fragment 72 to fragment 1, we are able to add that everything that is there said of the "inexperienced" is equally confirmed by fragment 2, where they are named anew ἀξύνετοι, "those who do not go along." With what do they not go along? With the λόγος, from which they are separated. The diverging-ones of fragment 72 are just such separated ones. It is thus the λόγος that must be our guiding thread for the reading of the fragments of Heraclitus (especially since these fragments are much less fragments in a genuine sense, than citations from a text now lost).

(The preceding remarks explain Heidegger's reservations a few months later during the 1966–67 winter semester Heraclitus seminar led by Eugen Fink at the University of Freiburg. The text of that seminar appeared in 1970 from Klostermann. Cf. especially pp. 179 f. "Your (i.e., Eugen Fink's) way of Heraclitus interpretation starts out from fire toward λόγος, my way of Heraclitus interpretation starts out from λόγος toward fire."[19])

September 8, 1966

> "Sleep in the hollow of my hand,
> olive tree, upon new earth,
> trust that beautiful will be the day,
> that morning, too, first found."[20]

Here, at the edge of the olive trees which nestle along the slope before us to the plain below where, off in the distance, not yet visible, the Rhône river flows, we begin again with fragment 2. Behind us rests a Delphic mountain range. This is the landscape of Rebanqué. Whoever finds the way there is a guest of the gods.

". . . (which is why it is necessary to direct oneself according to the ξυνόν, which means according to the κοινόν):

But from λόγος,which is the ξυνόν, they surely live, those who make up the great multitude, and such that each has his own opinion for himself."

Now we hear something more about the λόγος, though we already know from fragment 1 its name and its sameness with beings. The λόγος presents itself now as the ξυνόν. The commentary of Sextus Empiricus on the other hand says: ξυνόν means the same as κοινόν. But at exactly this point everything is questionable.

Heidegger says that behind what Heraclitus named ξυνόν, and even if this runs contrary to grammar, one must hear ξυνιέναι: a going together, the coming of one to the other. Whereas, the κοινόν is merely the καθόλον, the universal in the sense of what belongs equally to all despite differences; in the way that to be a living being, for example, is characteristic of frogs as well as of hounds. We could say that ξυνόν is the definition of ὄντα as ξυνιόντα, while the κοινόν is the determination of the ξυνόν from the standpoint of a thinking that is concerned with distinguishing universals from the individualities subordinate to them.

For Heraclitus, on the contrary, the "agreement," the co-belonging that lays in ξυνόν, is neither the universal nor the generic. What manner of belonging together does he then have in view? That of what essentially *is differing:* τὸ διαφερόμενον. This alone can *bring together,* in the Latin sense of *conferre, to move oneself* to the same side, *to turn* to it, thereby to belong in this way to the "agreement": in Greek, συμφέρεσθαι, in the sameness of διά and σύν. For example: day and night. There is no day "alone," nor night "apart by itself," but rather the co-belonging of day and night, which is their very being. If I say only "day," I do not yet know anything of the being of day. In order to think day, one must think it all the way to night and likewise the reverse. Night *is* day as the day that has set. To let day and night belong to each other, in this there is being just as much as λόγος. This is precisely what Hesiod could not understand, for he only saw the alternation of day and night, as he says in the *Theogony* (verse 751):

"The house never holds them both within."[21]

For Heraclitus it is precisely the opposite. The house of being is that of day-night taken together. Accordingly, he says in fragment 57:

"The teacher of the multitude, Hesiod, they hold him for a man of the deepest wisdom, he who did not recognize with respect to day and night: in truth it is one."

Coming back from this to fragment 72, it now says: the human lives everyday in relation to day and night. But, like Hesiod, he only notes their alternation or transformation. He does not see that this supposed alternation (transformation) is itself, more secretly, their very being. What truly *is,* is neither the one nor the other, but the co-belonging of the two as the concealed middle between them. But because the ἀξύνετοι who do not know the ξυνόν, turn away from²² that which they are essentially related to, everything appears to them in an alienating light. Unremittingly, the λόγος provides a measure which is not accepted. Thus:

Since the λόγος is in that which presences and its presencing, and in this respect assigns to each a measure, they live from it, the multitude, but nevertheless in such a way that each has an opinion for himself. They live from it, without knowing what they are talking about. They say "*is*" without knowing what "*is*" actually means.

Such is the case with the ἰδία φρόνησις, for which to be thirsty means nothing other than to be thirsty, to be hungry nothing other than to be hungry, since the day is only the day and the night nothing other than the night. Opposed to this is the ξυνόν, which we relate to the ξυνιέναι, and which Heraclitus understands even more boldly than us as: ξυν νόῳ λέγειν (fragment 114): to say the *sense* in agreement with νόος, or rather, to let it be in this agreement.

Those whose speech agrees with the νόος must become ever stronger by holding to the ξυνόν πάντων, to that wherein everything agrees — and not sway in any and all directions according to the wind of opinion, as happens to those who, instead of thinking, limit themselves to the gathering of information (ἱστορεῖν, fragment 35).

We shall conclude with two observations:

1) In everything for which λόγος provides the measure, it is indeed a matter of a διά, but λόγος is nonetheless never *dialectically* determined, that is, as the polarity of standing opposites. The διαφερόμενον of Heraclitus is much more the unfolding of contraries²³ and grounded in the inapparent character [*Unscheinbaren*] of λόγος. We explain:

The opposites exclude each another, while the contraries correspond to one another, in that they let one another reciprocally come forth, in the sense that:

> "The tide struggles with the pebble,
> and the light with the shade."²⁴

Just as Aeschylus says, "Dark and light are contrarily distributed to one another."²⁵ The conception of standing opposites presupposes the statement as *proposition*, within which they both appear through the play of negation. The investigation of the proposition is the business of logic, which is the art of preserving the λόγος from contradiction as a disagreement pushed to the extreme — at least as long as logic does not reverse its basic intention and become dialectic, for which contradiction, as Marx says, makes up the "font" of truth itself. It is characteristic of dialectic to play the two terms of a relation against each other, with the intent of bringing about a reversal in a situation previously determined by these terms. So for Hegel, as an example, day is the *thesis*, night is the *antithesis*, and so the spring board is found for a *synthesis* of day and night. It is a synthesis in the sense that the conflict of *being* and *nothing* is equalized by the appearance of *becoming*, which arises dialectically from their collision.

With Heraclitus, however, the reverse occurs. Instead of combining the opposites methodically, so that both terms of a relation play out against one another, he names the διαφερόμενον *as* the συμφερόμενον: "The God?—Day-Night!" This is the sense of φύσις. In other words, Heraclitus names a belonging to a singular presence of everything that separates itself from another, in order to turn all the more intimately to the other, in the sense that along the "country path": "Winter's storm encounters harvest's day, the agile excitation of Spring and the serene dying of Autumn meet, the child's game and the elder's wisdom gaze at each other. And in a unique harmony, whose echo the pathway carries with it silently here and there, everything is made gladsome. . . ."[26]

2) Human thinking itself, its νοεῖν, belongs to the λόγος and determines itself from this as ὁμολογεῖν (fragment 50). It was this, says Heidegger, that I attempted to show in a 1942 explanation of fragment 7 in a seminar for beginners. It is commonly translated thus:

"If all beings were to become smoke [καπνὸς γένοιτο], the nose would distinguish them."

In this, the sense of the verb γίνεσθαι is misunderstood, since, instead of the transformation of something into something else, it means here the presencing of it. Thus we translate:

"If being showed itself everywhere as smoke, then the nose would notice the difference."

One could not more humorously say that the faculty of knowledge is determined by the appearance of a being. With this, the proximity in which Heraclitus and Parmenides stand to one another is completely visible. Fragment 7, as we now understand it, is to a certain extent the Heraclitean conception of fragment 3 from Parmenides' poem:

"Indeed, the same is just as much thinking as being."

In summary:

1) With Heraclitus there is no dialectic—even if his word provides the impetus for this, since, in this sense, what began after him is literally that "which the morning *first* found."[27]

2) All thinking is "for the sake of being," which is certainly not to say that this would only be an object of thought.

September 9

"To the health of the snake"[28]

Today we are gathered at the house of the poet by the lavender fields. Already tomorrow we will depart from one another, but Heraclitus remains near to us, for we wish to read fragment 30 together.

"This κόσμος here, insofar as it is the same for everyone and everything, none of the gods and no man has brought forth, it always already was and it is and will be: inexhaustible living fire [ἀλλ' ἦν ἀεὶ καὶ ἔστιν καὶ ἔσται πῦρ ἀείζωον], kindled in measures and in measures going out."

We are already stopped by a first difficulty: how should the adverb ἀεί, which we have translated as "always already," be understood? Is it meant as an "eternal world," in the sense of Aristotle and the scholastics? Does it mean *aeternitas*? Or *sempiternitas*? We are reminded of Braque: "The everlasting versus the eternal." And furthermore: "The everlasting and the sound of its source."[29] However, the adverb appears related only to the imperfect ἦν, which is solely in reply to "has not brought it forth." It means that this world here has not been made, since it was already there at all times. Accordingly, the meaning is to be sought more in the direction of the eternal, since the everlasting is only first uttered afterwards, by means of the present [*Präsens*] and the future that follows upon it, and particularly by means of the second ἀεί in ἀείζωον, inexhaustible living. Here, however, eternity does not dominate time — something which, incidentally, is not explicitly called into question, but of which it is simply said that as far as one may go back, *this* "world" was already there. In "will be" there is an echo that corresponds precisely to the "is."[30]

We have said "world." This immediately calls to mind the idea of a great Whole. The effort to determine this will lead much later to Kantian "cosmology" along with the antinomies that develop from this — and then, even further, to the expeditions of space travelers ("cosmonauts"). Does Heraclitus really speak about this?

1) The verb κοσμέω, to which κόσμος belongs, means: to bring into an order. Without question, not in the sense of a mere distribution, but according to the way things belong to each other in the midst of a "common presence" ("*commune présence*"[31]), as day and night are joined to one another in the manner we saw. In this regard, κόσμος does not name something that would be larger than the other things and inside of which they all would find their space, but a way of being. Diels was also quite right when, in his presentation of the poem of Parmenides in 1897, he remarked, "For the philosophers of the fifth century, from Heraclitus on, κόσμος does not mean 'world.'"[32]

2) κόσμος is also just as much what the German word "*Zier*" [adornment] says: the gleam, the radiance, which was originally the same word as Zeus. By this, the light of Heaven is addressed. In this sense as well, the Cretans named those who shined at the head of the state κόσμοι.

3) There is yet a third meaning, quite common to Homer, that of decoration. It is also familiar to Pindar, for example, when he calls upon the "golden victory." Decoration as well as gold should not shine only

for itself, but, by its shining, show the one who wears it and upon whom it shines.

The concealed unity of this threefold sense constitutes the Heraclitean sense of "world,"—a sense which, on its way through Latin, is still preserved in the French *monde*, insofar as the opposite of *monde* is not some "other world," as one might unthinkingly represent it, but instead what is said by the adjective *immonde:* the impure.

— Since Heraclitus speaks with such a wealth of meaning, which he is nevertheless able to bring together in a single name, the poet says, he belongs in the company of the poets.

— It is so, Heidegger responds, because the fundamental relation of the Greek language to nature consists in leaving nature open in its radiance, and not, as one would have it in the modern era, in making its appearances easily calculable. Thus it names the κόσμος as older than the gods and men, which remain related back to it, since none of these at any time could have brought it forth.

This also explains, in a certain respect, in what way the κόσμος is a *fire* (πῦρ). Fire contains another threefold sense, insofar as it is simultaneously the rising flame, the brooding glow, and the radiating light, along with the richness of contrasts which this equivocation make possible. We, the completely different people of the modern era, as devotees of logic, believe the contrary, that a word is only first meaningful when it has just one meaning. But for Heraclitus precisely this manifold richness is the κόσμος. It never appears as something isolated, but shimmers ungraspably throughout everything. So we understand him in our reading of fragment 124: In comparison with the κόσμος, in its complete appearing as fire, "the most beautiful ordering of all is surely comparable to a heap of randomly spilled garbage." This means that the *inapparent joining together* of the κόσμος *is superior to every visible ordering*, even if it be the most beautiful possible (fragment 54).

And what follows now presents the most extreme opposition to this. As distinct from the "world" of Heraclitus, by the standard of which the plenitude of nature is offered to the inhabitants of this world, today a world dominates in which the decisive question runs: How do I have to represent nature in the sequence of its appearances to myself, so that I am in a position to make secure predictions about all and everything? The answer to this question is that it is compulsory to represent nature as a totality of energy particles of existing mass, the reciprocal movements of which are to be mathematically calculable. Descartes already says to the piece of wax that he holds before his eyes: "You are nothing other than an extended, flexible, and mutable thing," and thus I proclaim myself to know everything about you that there is to know of you. Someone from our circle says that in such a world there is room enough for everything, even for poetry, provided that it be something of a side concern, as is required there. To the seriousness of modern knowledge, there corresponds a conception of poetry as "pleasant sideline."[33]

— But, the poet asks, wherein lies the origin of this metamorphosis? From what "seed" was it able to sprout? And in whose name does the ban exist that strikes dumb the conversation of the "ones who belong to each other," that conversation in which, with a secret voice

"The fields say to me: stream
and the streams to me: fields?"[34]

— It is no more unthinkable, the thinker answered, than it is unachievable, that the human would no longer be there to correspond to what appears, but rather only to master what was an appearance for him in the beginning. Hence in the age of world impoverishment, a botanist sees in the blossoming of a flower only a sequence of chemical processes. Descartes actually takes no part in this, and what he sees in a flash was prepared long before him. Descartes was the first to see the lightning flash. That is what is decisive: that it was seen. Why it gave itself in this way and not another, of this we admittedly know nothing, at least in the sense where knowledge is the definition of a scientific law. Concerning this, I have risked speaking of the "destiny of being" as it had first addressed itself to Greek thinking at the beginning of *our* world. The Greeks stand under this destiny just as much as we do. Will we someday be in the position to think this on its own terms, instead of representing history as a succession of events? Therein lies the task of thinking, for which poetry is the "wholesome danger."[35] For poetry has not been unfaithful to the site of an inceptual upsurge, while on the contrary the becoming-philosophy of thinking—as well as of the world—determines the course upon which we today find ourselves: "losing the site," to adopt a word from Sophocles, however "well-deserving [indeed],"[36] as Hölderlin says, that we might think of ourselves.

Taking his leave from the cordial host who addresses him as a friend, Heidegger concludes the seminar by saying to us all in a heartfelt turn: "What remains essential is to continue along the same path without concern for any of the publicness around us."

August 30

This is the first session of the seminar. Consequently, Heidegger begins with a general remark on the work of the seminar. There can be no authority, since we work in common. We work in order to reach the matter itself [*Sache selbst*] which is in question. Thus the matter itself is the sole authority. On the basis of the text in question, the issue is to touch, and be touched by, the matter itself. The text is therefore ever only a means, not an end.

In our case, the issue is Hegel: we must therefore begin a confrontation [*Auseinandersetzung*] with Hegel, so that Hegel *speaks* to us. To let him speak for himself, and not to correct what Hegel has to say with what we know. In this way alone can one prevent the danger of personal interpretation.

This is why, in a genuine seminar, the teacher is the one who learns the most. For this, it is not required that he instruct the others what the text means, but instead that he listen rightly to the text.

In the seminar it is important to question relentlessly. By their questions, the students are to support the inquiry of the teacher. Nothing is ever to be merely *believed;* everything must be experienced. Clearly, then, the work cannot be measured by the amount covered.

Heidegger mentions that in Marburg his way of working aroused criticism. In the beginning, the students said: during the course of an entire semester, we did not once come out of Plato's *Sophist.* . . . With respect to our seminar, Heidegger continued, we cannot be sure of working through more than a few lines of the text. But one thing is certain, if all this is assumed, then we would be able to read Hegel's whole book. That, he says, is the secret of the seminar.

He then moved to a quick description of the historical atmosphere at the time of the composition of the *Differenzschrift*.[37] It took place during Hegel's time at Frankfurt (Hegel remained in Frankfurt until January 1801). At that time, Hölderlin lived in the vicinity, in Bad Homburg, and the two friends were in contact. However, this proximity is problematic. For the poet, already at that time, and despite all appearances of dialectic that his essays might exhibit, had already gone through and broken the speculative dialectic—whereas Hegel was in the process of establishing it. Heidegger notes that this could be a question for the upcoming days.

What gave rise to the text? The book of a contemporary, Reinhold. Born in Vienna, Reinhold studied with the Jesuits, went into philosophy, and turned to Protestantism. He was a joyous and brave man. When he was called to Kiel, Fichte succeeded him as chair in Jena. Hegel treated him far too poorly.

Shortly after the publication, on October 3, 1801, Schelling wrote to Fichte: "Just recently, a book came out from a truly superior mind. . . ."[38]

After having circumscribed the exterior, we now need to "leap into the matter itself." On this point, Heidegger begins with a citation from Hegel: "a torn sock is better than a mended one . . . "[39] and asks, why is that so? A moment of hesitation follows, for the auditors know another version of that same sentence. Heidegger explains that the sentence just cited was "corrected" by the printer into the one we know. Let us return to Hegel's citation and ask how he could have written this. For it is plain that it is the contrary that seems the case. From a strictly formal point of view, one can say that common sense is reversed, stood on its head.

In order to understand, Heidegger says, one must see phenomeno-logically. He thus invites us to the first exercise of phenomenological "kindergarten." To tear apart [*zer-reissen*] means: to tear into two parts, to separate: to make two out of one. If a sock is torn, then the sock is no longer present-at-hand—but note: precisely not *as* a sock. In fact, when I have it on my foot, I see the "intact" sock precisely not *as* a sock. On the contrary, if it is torn, then THE sock appears with more force through the "sock torn into pieces."

In other words, what is lacking in the torn sock is the UNITY of the sock. However, this lack is paradoxically the most positive, for this Unity in being-torn is *present* [*gegenwärtig*] as a *lost* unity. This is the point of departure from which to access Hegel's text, but not without Heidegger insisting that the "analysis" undertaken be reenacted ("real-ized" in Cézanne's sense), and not simply presented conceptually.

Page 12, l. 6 ff./89: "*Dichotomy* [*Entzweiung*]," underlined by Hegel, "is the source of the *need for philosophy*." In order to stress that Hegel starts from the dichotomy, as what is originally experienceable and experi-enced, this is brought into relation with the sentence from p. 13, l. 30 ff./90: "Opposites such as spirit and matter, soul and body, faith and understanding, freedom and necessity, etc., used to be important; and in more limited spheres . . . " until the passage concerning the radical opposition of "absolute subjectivity and absolute objectivity."[40]

This sentence states negatively that all the attempts to suppress the "tearing" [*Zerrissenheit*] must be abandoned—insofar as the "tearing" is what basically remains and must so remain. Why? Answer: as we saw above, it is only in the tearing that the Unity, as absent, can appear. "In the tearing," Heidegger says, "there always reigns unity or a necessary conjoining, that is, a *living* unity."

With this central idea of a "*living unity*," one can now read the sen-tence on page 14, l. 9/91, which, according to Heidegger, governs every-thing: "When the power of conjoining. . . ." This sentence is a commentary on the one from page 12/89 on the dichotomy as source of the need for philosophy. One therefore notes:

1) That the scission [*Ent-zweiung*] lies in the movement of the *"Ent-,"* that is to say, it is a departure whereby something *leaves* something. In scission there are two that *separate* into two.

2) That this scission takes place through a lack of conjoining (*Vereinigung*).

In this respect, a remark on the translation of *"Vereinigung"*: *"unification"* ["unifying, becoming one"] does not work. How is it then to be understood? First by noting that, once unfolded, "the power of conjoining" is an indication of the Absolute. In this respect, Heidegger recalls that from its inception, thought thinks within the dimension of *unity*.

He raises the question of why this is the case. This question will be taken up later.

We then return to conjoining in order to indicate its difference from *unification*. In the conjoining — insofar as it is the work of the Absolute — *the oppositions do not disappear*. There is a unity of opposites that remain as opposites. What, then, is this conjoining? It is the power that holds the opposites together *for one another:* in this holding together, there is no longer room for the autonomy, or separatism, of the opposites each for itself (which characterizes the scission).

This allows one to read the preceding sentence (p.14, l. 2 ff./91) where the idea of "a necessary dichotomy" arises, which is in fact necessary if all position is necessarily counter-position, and thus creates duality.

By reading the two sentences together, one enters into Hegel's thinking: everything lies in the antagonism of a positing activity — and consequently a counter-positing activity — with the force that is capable of holding the unity of the two together, and this is due to the *positing* of unity, which for its part brings forth what is counter-posited [*das Entgegen-Gesetzte*], which also must be "conjoined" and so forth . . .

But is it really the case of a "so forth"? Here appears the last theme discussed today: that of the *infinite*.

It is important to see that "infinite" can mean *"ad infinitum,"* in other words: to see the "endless" character of the finite. But then one has what Hegel calls the bad infinite. The opposite of this is the true infinite, where infinite means: in-finite, i.e., the sublation of the finite. The true infinite is the one where the finite is *abandoned*. That infinite is no longer the lack of ends, but rather the power of conjoining itself.

August 31

At first Heidegger takes up again the sense of Hegel's sentence: "A mended sock is better than a torn one, not so with self-consciousness [*Selbstbewusstsein*]."[41]

In order to properly understand this sentence, one needs to bear in mind the two-fold sense of the word *"self consciousness"* in Hegel. On the one hand, the word designates ordinary consciousness in its non-thematic relation to objects,[42] and on the other hand, the problem of the *ego cogito* which has stood at the center of modern thought since Descartes. Hegel means to say: Ordinary thinking does not mean that a torn sock is better than a mended sock. However, as soon as one takes *"self consciousness"* in the sense of the dialectical-reflexive thinking, one needs to understand that dialectical-reflexive thinking gathers both sound common sense and its truth (its philosophical thematization) into a higher unity.[43]

Two questions are then posed:

1. If the "scission" is the source of the need for philosophy, if philosophy arises as soon as life has become torn, *what is the driving force of the dichotomy?*

2. If philosophy is not a piecing-together and if the tearing is necessary, *then can one speak of a unity before the tearing?*

For the answer to the second question, Heidegger refers to Chapter 1 of Aristotle's *Physics*. Whoever wants to enter into philosophy must pass through this book, which can replace entire libraries of philosophical works.

The answer to the first question is rendered easier by returning to Hegel's statement which refers the dichotomy to its most simple and essential example: "Opposites such as spirit and matter, soul and body, faith and understanding, freedom and necessity, etc. used to be important; and in more limited spheres they appeared in a variety of other guises. The whole weight of human interests hung upon them. With the progress of culture they have passed over into such forms as the opposition of Reason and sensibility, intelligence and nature and, with respect to the universal concept, of *absolute subjectivity* and *absolute objectivity*" (p. 13/90, our emphasis).[44]

How do we get to this separation, this dichotomy between the subject and the object? How does one emerge in relation to the other? This question presupposes an earlier stage when the dichotomy had not yet occurred. This earlier stage, for Hegel, is the Greek world.

What is in fact the driving force of the subject-object dichotomy? It is the quest for absolute certainty. Such a quest, which is born out of an interpretation of truth as certainty, appears historically with Descartes' first *Meditation*. With Descartes, man as *ego cogito* becomes the distinctive ὑποκείμενον, the *subjectum* (in the medieval sense) — the *fundamentum inconcussum*. Henceforth, nature only appears as an Object for a Subject.

As a historical prelude to this advent, one can note that the quest for certainty appears first in the domain of faith, as the search for the certainty of salvation (Luther), then in the domain of physics as the search for the *mathematical* certainty of nature (Galileo) — a search long prepared by the nominalist separation of words and things in the field of language (William of Ockham). By evacuating the concept of reality, Ockham's formalism renders possible the project of a mathematical key to the world.

Hence the question: Is it possible to grasp in one concept, with a compelling necessity, the unity of mathematical certainty and the certainty of salvation?

Heidegger answers that it is the *assurance* (mastery, availability, security) each time sought that brings together these two apparently independent matters. In the quest for mathematical certainty, what is sought is the assurance of man in nature, in the *sensible;* in the quest for the certainty of salvation, what is sought is the assurance of man in the *supra-sensible* world.

The origin of the dichotomy is thus the mutation of truth into certainty, to which corresponds the priority given to the entity man in the sense of the *ego cogito,* its rise to the position of *subject.* Henceforth, nature becomes *object* (*ob-jectum*), the object being nothing other than "what is thrown over against me" [*das mir Entgegengeworfene*]. As soon as the ego becomes the absolute Subject, all other beings become objects for it, for example, in the form of perception (this is the point of departure for the "Object" in the Kantian sense). What is decisive is that the subject-object distinction plays entirely in the dimension of subjectivity. This dimension is characterized by Hegel through the expression *consciousness.* "Consciousness" is the sphere of subjectivity. Consciousness, that is, "seeing everything together," *co-agere.* All of Hegel's essential terms in the text in question relate to consciousness.

The paragraphs devoted to Descartes in *Being and Time* represent the first attempt to exit the prison of consciousness, or rather to no longer enter it. It is in no way a question of restoring realism against idealism, for realism, by limiting itself to the assurance that a world exists for the subject, remains dependent upon Cartesianism. It is rather a question of attempting to think the *Greek* sense of the ἐγώ.

Returning from consciousness to the dichotomy, Heidegger introduces a new statement by Hegel: "When the power of conjoining vanishes from the life of men and the opposites lose their living connection and reciprocity and gain independence, the need of philosophy arises" (p. 14/91).

Two words here need to be clarified: need and philosophy. What does the expression "need of philosophy" mean? Viewed grammatically, we have before us a genitive. This genitive is usually understood as a *genitivus objectivus:* when the power of conjoining disappears from the life of men, these men feel the need to philosophize. But what does "need" mean? The word has a negative connotation. To need something is to experience together the absence, lack and necessity of that thing; it means to be "in need, in distress" with respect to something. But the word also has a positive sense: to need something means to set out for something, to work for something, to take pains to obtain something.

Should we understand that something is in need of philosophy, or, on the contrary, is it philosophy that is in need of something? Is it a *genetivus subjectivus* or a *genitivus objectivus?* It is, Heidegger says, a *genetivus subjectivus.* Hegel wants to show what philosophy needs in order for it to be authentic philosophy.

But what does philosophy need? Since its inception, since the ἕν πάντα of Heraclitus and the ἕν of Parmenides, philosophy does not think the many, but rather the manifold, and the way in which it is unified. Philosophy needs the ἕν. This is why philosophy can and should assist the power of conjoining. In the expression, "need of philosophy," the genitive is *at once both genitivus subjectivus and objectivus.* It is only if one understands what philosophy needs, absolute and total unity, that one can then understand why the need of philosophy arises.

There is a need for unity, because unity is never given immediately; otherwise, everything would be engulfed in Schelling's "night where all cows are black." In the midst of the highest dichotomy, unity is constantly restored. This is why Hegel writes: ". . . the necessary dichotomy is One factor in life. Life eternally forms itself by setting up oppositions, and totality at the highest pitch of living energy is only possible through its own re-establishment out of the deepest fission" (p. 14, top/91).

After this has been presented, Heidegger recalls the Hegelian meaning of the word Science [*Wissenschaft*]. Hegel uses the word in Fichte's sense. The "System of Science" that includes both the *Phenomenology* and the *Logic* together, is the system of philosophy. "Science" is the name for philosophy having become absolute knowledge, namely of the subject which knows itself as *fundamentum inconcussum.*

Husserl at times would vacillate between the ordinary sense of the word and its Hegelian sense, as can be seen in the *Crisis.*[45]

Heidegger then raises a few questions. If the need of philosophy is what philosophy needs in order to be philosophy, what then is philosophy? Its essence is glimpsed on the basis of a recollection of Heraclitus' and Parmenides' ἕν: philosophy is an attempt at conjoining. Listening to the tradition of philosophy, that is, to metaphysics, we learn that philosophy treats of the being of beings. What is then the relation between the ἕν and the being of beings? The relation between the ἕν and οὐσία? Since being is not an empty word, a mere exchangeable currency, but always concretely apprehended as present [*Gegenwart*], as presence [*Anwesenheit*], what accordingly is the relation between presence and unity?

Jean Beaufret says that the difficulty of this question appears quite clearly in regard to Aristotle's philosophy. With Aristotle, this πολλαχῶς λεγόμενον, which is being, appears in four ways:

1. According to the categories;
2. According to the relation δύναμις-ἐνέργεια;
3. According to the relation οὐσία-συμβεβηκός;
4. As ἀληθές and ψεῦδος.

What is the unity of being, that single realm? Aristotle does not say.

Heidegger retrieves Aristotle's example, restricting himself to the third guise of being. What is the relation between συμβεβηκός and presencing?

To answer this question, one must first attempt to avoid thinking the συμβεβηκός on the basis of the scholastic interpretation of the opposition substance-accident, as expressed in a grammatical theory where the relation between accident and substance is nothing other than that of predicate to subject in a statement.

If one takes a rose, one is able to distinguish at a glance the necessary and the accidental συμβεβήκοτα. One sees, on the basis of the rose-being—that is, of the presence of the rose—that color does not constitute its essence, but instead the multiplicity of petals. Understood on the basis of the presencing of the rose, the συμβεβηκός is in a certain way understood on the basis of the past: the petals of the rose have *always already* arrived with the presence of the rose (meaning of the Greek perfect tense).

But this is seen only thanks to another gathering, that of *Logos*. Logos always projects itself toward things that appear in *their* gathering. For *Greek* thought, the presencing of the human is the opening inception for the oppositional presencing of the World.

Now, where does the encounter take place between that which presences and the being whose mode of presence is a self-opening for the welcoming of this presence? Where, except in ἀλήθεια? This is why ἀλήθεια cannot be translated by "truth."

September 1

For some time the session took the form of a "Sunday seminar"—concerning which nothing in particular is to be reported.[46]

After Heidegger invoked for us the figure of his teacher Husserl through anecdotes showing us the extent of the passion that moved the author of *Logical Investigations,* we retained only this remark:

For Husserl, there was something which did not exist, namely the deep meaning of history as Tradition (as that which delivers us), in the sense where Plato is here, Aristotle is here, and they speak to us, they are present [*gegenwärtig*] to us and must be present to us.

This brings us back to Hegel.

Heidegger had in an earlier hour familiarized us with the expression "need of philosophy." The task was then to understand this genitive as *genitivus objectivus* and *genitivus subjectivus,* whereby the *gentivus subjectivus* appeared predominant. Yesterday[47] the entire investigation concerned the word "philosophy." To understand the word "philosophy" rigorously, we must anticipate and consider this passage from page 25/ 103 (tm), which, in a certain respect, contains everything: "Philosophy, as a totality of knowledge produced by reflection, becomes a system, that is, an organic whole of concepts, whose highest law is not the understanding, but Reason."

In this sentence, where the word *"ground"* is patently missing, every word is significant and calls for a commentary. The words to comment upon are: Reflection, Production, Totality, Knowledge, System, Organic, Concept, Law, Understanding, Reason.

The basic word is *System.* It is taken from the Greek where we hear:

1) σύν, together, the gathering. This is the "power of conjoining."

2) τίθημι, to posit—that is, the positing, determined by Kant, of Being as objectivity.

In thinking this notion of system, we are able to measure the distance that separates Hegel from Kant. Kant speaks of system in the "Doctrine of Method," nevertheless, a system is only possible after Fichte. This possibility is brought to its highest degree of completion by Hegel himself, since, at the end of his life, Schelling again fell outside the system. Thus in philosophy there is no system in the strict sense other than that of these two thinkers.

That there is strictly speaking no system in Kant (and even less in Aristotle and Aquinas) can be experienced by reading this passage from the *Critique of Pure Reason:*

> Unconditioned necessity, which we so indispensably require as the last bearer of all things, is for human reason the veritable *abyss.* Eternity itself, in all its terrible sublimity, as depicted by a Haller, is far from making the same overwhelming impression on the mind; for it only *measures* the duration of things, it does not *support* them. We cannot put aside, and yet also cannot endure the thought, that a being, which we represent to ourselves as supreme amongst all possible beings, should, as it were, say to itself: 'I am from eternity to eternity, and outside me there is nothing save what is through my will, *but whence then am I?*' All support here fails us; and the *greatest* perfection, no less than the *least* perfection, is unsubstantial and baseless for the merely speculative reason, which makes not the least effort to retain either the one or the other, and feels indeed no loss in allowing them to vanish entirely.[48]

This text, where God Himself, as it were, appears as abyss, is taken from the chapter: "The Impossibility of a Cosmological Proof of the Existence of God." The impossibility in question appears at the same time as that of the system itself, if we question this text more closely.

The text begins by naming the system in the subordinate clause: "Unconditioned necessity, which we so indispensably require as the last bearer of all things" and designates it as "the veritable abyss for human reason." The abyss of the system, as Kant conceives of it, lies in that speculative reason finds nothing to establish in regard to what is essential to the production of a system, as ultimate ground of everything. Indeed, for speculative reason, this is always only an Idea (in the sense of the *Critique of Pure Reason*, where "idea" is opposed to "intuition" and "concept"). Speculatively, it is only an idea of reason, and in this sense it is ungrounded, abyssal. Thus we can also say that in this text we explicitly encounter Kant's renunciation of a speculative system.

Now, it is precisely here—if we let history speak—that everything is turned upside down, while Kant, still living, witnessed with horror what began to take place with Fichte. We can say that Fichte and Hegel are looking for a ground where for Kant there could only be an abyss. In thirty years everything will be reversed, so much so that in his Berlin discourse we can say that Hegel spoke in a way diametrically opposed to the text of the *Critique of Pure Reason* we just read. The several stages that led to this can be briefly summarized as follow:

1) Fichte, insofar as for his part he knows the answer to the question left unanswered by Kant: "But where do I come from?" The answer is I = I.

2) The Hegel of the *Differenzschrift*—this is what we have begun to grasp directly by paying attention to the difficult passage of page 17/94: "The form that the need of philosophy would assume, if it were to be expressed as a presupposition, allows for a transition from the need of philosophy to the *instrument of philosophizing, to reflection* as Reason."

This sentence brings us before *reflection as Reason.* Let us note, first, that with Hegel the meaning of the word reflection changes. It designates here the later dialectical thinking. Later, Hegel would reserve this term for the understanding alone and characterize philosophies other than his as "philosophies of reflection."

If we question this phrase, we see that speculative reason—of which Kant emphasized its finitude and powerlessness—straight away appears fully capable of being the instrument of philosophical activity, that is, of the work that produces the system. Speculation becomes autonomous. This unveils a power of speculation that was impossible for Kant. However, the whole problem is to explicate the phrase. This is why the task set for today (September 2) will consist in more precisely determining reflection in general, then in distinguishing reflection as understanding, and finally in indicating the extent to which reflection is reason.

September 2

Heidegger opens the work of September 2 by restating that the correct comportment to the *work of the seminar* avoids the merely historical questioning and protects itself against taking the text as a pretext for questions that would be "ours."

The second question raised in the last hour, but left undeveloped, is then taken up again: "Can one speak of a unity before the tearing?" The first question (concerning the driving force of the dichotomy) was treated in a historical-philosophical manner. The second question now requires of us a pre-philosophical approach. However, to pose this question on the basis of our reading of Hegel, Heidegger again relies on the sentence from page 14/91: "When the power of conjoining, etc. . . ." The question is then:

When the power of conjoining disappears, what is experienced in this type of experience along with the disappearance of the unity? It is the unity itself. Thus one not only can but must speak of unity *before* the dichotomy. Certainly, the answer: "unity" is a theoretical one. Now the question requires of us a pre-philosophical approach. Heidegger invites us to such a preparation, phenomenological in a more authentic sense.

Let us take this example: "Night falls, it is no longer day," and in this particular region where night brusquely succeeds the day, in such a way that the example directs us to the experience of a relation of strong opposition. *Where* does the passage from day to night take place? "In what place" does it take place? What is the unity whose splitting-in-two this transition presents? What is the Same in which the day passes into the night? In such an experience, human beings stand in relation with something which is neither day nor night, even if not expressly thematized.

And that is? World, light, space, time, etc., these all too general answers attest to a phenomenological difficulty. The example seemed too massive. So, another example: a pot which breaks apart. To be able to see the parts (as such) there must be a relation to the unity. If we consider that, since Heraclitus, this unity is called ἕν, and that, since this inception, the One is the other name for being, then we are referred back to the understanding of being spoken of in *Being and Time.*

At this juncture, Heidegger recalls the criticisms that followed the publication of *Being and Time.* Heidegger was accused of having derived "being" from "is" and then of having developed his "philosophy" from this "abstraction." To these critiques, he answers still today that "being is not an abstraction drawn from the 'is'; rather, I can say 'is' only in the openness of Being."

We return to tearing, understood on the basis of what is torn apart, of the rift [*Riß*]; the experience of which is only possible in a certain "return to" unity: this is so much the case that in Hegel it *must* be there. In fact, page 16/93: "In the struggle of the understanding with Reason the understanding has strength only to the degree that Reason forsakes itself."[49] If we understand Reason in the Kantian sense (as faculty of principles, faculty of unity), reason is renounced in favor of the understanding, the power of conjoining withdraws before the Understanding, the particularity of which is the stabilization of opposites. The unity has not disappeared but remains in the background. If we over-interpret, we could say that reason—as faculty of unity, in other words, the perceiving of being—yields to the ordering of entities, so that in this withdrawal of Reason behind the production of the Understanding the ontological difference is at stake.

Returning to page 16/93, we continue the reading: "The need of philosophy *can* be called the *presupposition* of philosophy if philosophy, which begins with itself, has to be furnished with some sort of vestibule." And, two lines further, "What is called the presupposition of philosophy is nothing else but *the need that has come to utterance.*" Heidegger asks, what does "come to utterance" here mean? The expression, in the following sentence: "Once uttered, the need is posited for reflection," indicates that the proper rendering for "come to utterance" would be: "expressed in speech, but not accomplished in philosophy." The need is only expressed in speech, it is not satisfied in this.

From this, Reason opens itself to reflection which expresses in speech the need for philosophy, in order to show which form philosophy now assumes. Everything on page 16/93 appears *necessary,* like an apparatus or a means to pass from the need of philosophy (as a "discourse about") to the instrument of philosophy. Reason's presentation to the understanding of the task of philosophy, a task that the understanding cannot accomplish, will reveal the lack of the instrument—and thus the passage to it.

More slowly: The first presupposition unfolds itself, a signal that it is a reflection of the understanding that establishes opposites. These are, on the one hand, the Absolute itself, and on the other hand, the totality of the dichotomies. The other presupposition states that the exit of consciousness out of the totality *would take* the form of a dichotomy into being and non-being, concept and being, finitude and infinitude. "Concept" is taken here as "representation of something in general," and "being" as "objectivity." From what unity is the dichotomy in these examples a dichotomy? For being and non-being, it is becoming; for the concept and being, it is the Absolute; for the finite and the infinite, it is Life.

For the understanding, absolute synthesis is what it can neither grasp nor determine; it is the formless, as opposed to the understanding's determinations. For reason, speaking to the understanding from the perspective of the dichotomy, philosophy nevertheless appears as the conjoining of both presuppositions (this is indicated by the first "however": "the task of philosophy, *however,* consists in . . ."[50]). These presuppositions are not separated from reason, as indicated by the second "however" (in the sentence: "It is clumsy, however, . . ."[51]). This absolute synthesis is the last thing that the understanding, within *its* horizon and unsettled by reason, is able to perceive; this is the "task" of the understanding, concerning which it can (merely) "speak."

What have we gained, in sum, working through this page? What emerges is both the lack of an *instrument* for the task of philosophy and, in the two presuppositions and their unification, the theme of specula- tion. What the understanding is incapable of understanding is how the limitations at the heart of reason, abolished because they are referred to the absolute, are to that very extent *produced* in this "abolishing" relation itself. This is why Heidegger refers to that passage from page 33/112 (tm): "The need of philosophy can appease itself by simply penetrating to the principle of nullifying all fixed oppositions and connecting the limited to the Absolute."

There is "appeasement," that is, first, "peace," because only the *fixities* disappear, while the *oppositions* appear in their vitality.

In conclusion, reading the text and translation of page 17/94, which closes the session, Heidegger makes two preliminary remarks concern- ing Hegel's terms:

—The first bears on the beginning of the second paragraph of "Reflection as Instrument of Philosophizing" and focuses on the expres- sion "Reflection in *isolation*"[52] which is better understood as: "the isolat- ing reflection."

—The second bears on the "standing" [*Bestehen*][53] which closes that same paragraph, a term that was constantly used by Hegel, but without analysis, as if we were running against a certain limit within Hegelian thought.

September 4

Heidegger opens the session with a remark concerning the word *con- cept* [*Begriff*], encountered on page 16/93 together with the word *being*: "concept and being." He clarifies its meaning on the basis of Kant's *rep- resentation* [*Vorstellung*], whose meaning is two-fold:

—The particular representation (the intuition)—for instance, of this book;

—The representation in general (the concept)—for instance, of the book as such.

Heidegger specifies that the issue is the latter sense, representation of all objects, of the object as object.

We are then led back to what was the focus of the discussion at the beginning of the preceding session: an interpretation of the text that is not only historical but that also engages the question of being. Heideg- ger now asks whether it strictly can be said that the question of being is the question of metaphysics. The answer is that if indeed metaphysics inquires into the being of beings ("What is a being as a being?"), it nevertheless does not inquire into being itself. When one poses a question, one questions in regard to . . . ; the place from where one questions grounds both the point of departure and the scope of the questioning. But this should be seen in an example, in a phenomenological manner.

Starting from a question concerning the color of the leaves on a tree that we see in the garden before us, we then ask about the point of departure which gives the question its scope. Further, no longer considering the color of this particular tree, but color as color, Heidegger asks: "What is proper to all colors?" He underlines how such a question, in which the matter is taken *as it is,* is different from Husserl's, who sought to clarify the constitution of the object in consciousness by analyzing the phenomenological sense of the sensible given, in other words, by phenomenologizing the Kantian analysis of the anticipations of perception. Since we undertake no reduction to consciousness, but take into view the matter itself, we are led to answer: "Any color, as color, is extended." Then, paying attention to sound—as a sort of counterexample—it appears that sound is in space in two ways: on the one hand, it comes from a place; on the other hand, it traverses and measures space. Yet sound as such is not *extended* in space, it is extended only in time.

Heidegger then returns to his first question, which is that of the *provenance* and *direction of inquiry* for metaphysics. Metaphysics starts from beings, raises itself to being, and then returns to beings as beings and clarifies them on the basis of the light of being. To explain this return to beings, an example is proposed of a question which starts from nature in the broadest sense and asks: "What is nature?" What it is cannot be determined by an answer distinct from it. *"Energeia"* is not outside of, or behind, what is, like some higher being; it is *in* the being. The difficulty only remains of determining the relation between beings and being.

However, if one speaks of metaphysics in this way, one can do so only insofar as metaphysics inquires into being in regard to how it determines beings as beings. Now, in another sense, the question of being is *entirely other.* It does not inquire into being insofar as it determines beings as beings; it inquires into being as being.

If the ontological difference which appears here is the most dangerous matter for thinking, it is because it always represents being, within the horizon of metaphysics, as a being. Now, the question of beings as beings, that is, the metaphysical question, means something other than the question of being as being. This can be stated negatively, by saying that the question of being as being does not somehow raise the being of beings to the second power.

The problem then arises of formulating the question of being in relation to Hegel. This can only be done on the basis of Hegel's text itself, from the place where, if not the answer, at least the difficulty of such an answer is formulated—from the place which attempts to state how the need of philosophy (that is, its questioning concerning beings) is appeased. The appeasement of the need thus contains the answer to the question concerning the being of beings. On page 33/112 of the text we read: "The need of philosophy can appease itself by simply penetrating. . . ."[54] Philosophy, that is, metaphysics, thus reaches the answers to its questions when the Absolute is grasped as Absolute. This task is named on page 17/94: "The Absolute is to be posited in reflection."

In the most usual sense of the word "reflection," we hear in this word the Latin *re-flexere*. What is proper to reflection is a turning-back upon itself. Towards what? Towards the *ego*. The essence of the *"cogitare"* is grasped by Descartes in the formulation: c*ogito me cogitare*. It lets the *cogito* appear as a *"me cogitare,"* and the *ego*, insofar as it is *cogitans*, appear as a *cogitatum*, as object. In the Kantian language of the transcendental deduction, it is expressed so: "It must be possible for the *I think* to accompany all my representations."[55] The title of § 17 of the same section is: "The Principle of the Synthetic Unity is the Supreme Principle of all Employment of the Understanding"; all *"cogitare"* is consequently an *ego cogito me cogitare*.

What Kant says of transcendental apperception is said in regard to the finite essence of man, and this relation of thought to unity is grasped by Hegel alone. This principle of conjoining at the level of the finite understanding is absolutized in such a way that Hegel brings the power of conjoining to absolute power: what is finite with man becomes the infinite Absolute.

In this respect, Heidegger notes that the infinite should not be understood in terms of the "end-less" of the understanding, but instead as the sublation of the finite. He also indicates that the first step taken in this elevation is accomplished by Fichte's sentence: "The Ego posits itself." To the extent that the Ego posits itself as self-positing, it also posits the non-Ego as identity. However, when the principle is, "I posit myself as self-positing," and thus simultaneously posit the non-Ego, what is the highest principle? This principle, or the principle of identity? Between Fichte's principle and the principle of identity, which one has priority over the other? Is formal logic the foundation of transcendental logic, or is transcendental logic the foundation of formal logic?

Where in Kant the problem of transcendental apperception is brought to its highest point, the relation to unity sets the standard. Such a question, which in Kant takes place at the level of the finite understanding, runs through all of transcendental idealism. The difference and relation between formal Logic and transcendental Logic is the difference and relation between an ordinary principle and a speculative one.

Returning to Hegel's statement, "The Absolute is to be posited in reflection. . . ," Heidegger recalls that Reflection is the movement that turns back upon itself, to the self, which is actually thinking insofar as it reflects. Hence the general sense of thinking for reflection is as follows: to reflect is to think about something, to think a thought. Reflection is thus a mediation between the one who thinks and what he or she thinks: consciousness becomes self-consciousness. Heidegger ends the session by drawing our attention to the fact that Hegel does *not* say: "We are to reflect on the Absolute," but rather: "The Absolute is to be reflected."

September 5

The question that led the September 5 seminar was that of the *danger of the ontological difference*. "The danger is that, within the horizon of metaphysics, the difference leads to representing being as a being. However, when Aristotle defines being as ἐνέργεια, or Plato as εἶδος, ἐνέργεια and εἶδος are not beings. Metaphysics struggles against defining being as a being, however tempted it is to do so." Hence the two stages of the seminar, to answer the questions:
  1) What does "ontological difference" mean?
  2) What fundamental experience determined Aristotle to experience beings (in their being) as ἐνέργεια, Plato as εἶδος, Kant as Object?

What does "ontological difference" mean?
  It can be understood in two ways: a) First, the expression "ontological difference" appears to be constructed like the expression: "the green tree"; "ontological" is therefore the adjective of the substantive "difference." From this first perspective, it would be the very difference between being and beings that is ontological, as one says of a leaf that it is green. b) But, and this is the second way of understanding, what if it were somehow the difference between being and beings itself that carried ontology along and rendered it possible as the fundamental discipline of metaphysics?
  This second understanding is confirmed by the fact that all metaphysics indeed moves within the difference (this is constantly stressed, in particular by Aquinas), but that no metaphysics recognizes this difference as difference in the dimension that it unfolds.
  The question thus arises: what is the relation between ontology and the difference of being from beings? Can metaphysics take up this question, since metaphysics, as ontology, is grounded upon this difference itself? Can difference, which renders metaphysics as metaphysics possible, be taken into consideration by the fundamental discipline of metaphysics, that is, ontology? In logical terms, can the consequence take into view the governing principle? No. I can, from the perspective of

the foundation, determine a consequence, but the reverse is impossible. The horizon in which the ontological difference is treated cannot appear as an explicit theme for ontology.

To take an example, in Aristotle, and for him, the ontological difference would refer to the pair θεῖον-ἐνέργεια. But τὸ θεῖον cannot be a term of the difference. It is named, τὸ τιμιώτατον ὄν, the being with the highest dignity. Hence, τὸ θεῖον is an explicitly ontic determination. Of the two terms—τὸ θεῖον, ἡ ἐνέργεια—only the latter, ἡ ἐνέργεια, has a relation to the ontological difference. It is this term that names being (τὸ εἶναι), and it is on the understanding of εἶναι as ἐνέργεια that Aristotle's ontology is founded.

To understand this misinterpretation (among others) of Aristotle, according to which τὸ θεῖον would be a term of the difference on which ontology would be founded, we need to make a leap beyond the intertwining of the questions, a leap into medieval theology. God is posited as *Summum Ens*, and *Summum Ens* is interpreted as *actus purus essendi*. How is this interpretation possible? What is the connection between the relation of *Summum Ens* and *Actus purus* to the Aristotelian relation between τὸ θεῖον and ἐνέργεια? Why does ἐνέργεια become *actualitas*? Because ἔργον and ἐνέργεια are understood by the Romans on the basis of AGERE, "to make" in an ontic sense. The name for such an ontic "making" is CREATIO. This is why the *Summum ens* becomes CREATOR, and all ENS is ENS CREATUM (or INCREATUM). Having on the one hand reduced ἐνέργεια to the ontic determination of *actualitas*, and, on the other hand, with Aquinas, having identified the *Summum Ens* with the *Ipsum esse*, ontology suppresses every possibility for a question of being. The entirety of modern philosophy is burdened by this ontic stamp inherited from the Christian ontology of the middle ages. To restore philosophy to its own essence means to purge it of its Christian element, and to do this out of concern for the Greek element—not for its own sake, but insofar as it is the origin of philosophy.

What then is properly fundamental for ontology in ἐνέργεια? In what sense does ἐνέργεια refer to the ontological difference? Through what fundamental experience does Aristotle arrive at ἐνέργεια?

A fundamental experience is the way in which beings are experienced. Thus Kant experiences beings as nature, in Newton's sense. And nature is here that which is, since, in the purview of Cartesian thinking, truth is certainty.

The experience of beings in their being as ἐνέργεια situates Aristotle in relation to Plato. For example, what is a chair for Plato? A μὴ ὄν, an "un-being" (in contrast with οὐκ ὄν, sheer non-being). Now, what is the ontological character of this μὴ ὄν? Plato names this deficient mode of being εἴδωλον, idol, distinguishing it from εἶδος, while nevertheless connecting them. Εἶδος is what shows itself, what one sees. The

εἴδωλον, without which I could not reach the εἶδος of the table, indicates that the εἶδος of the table is *obscured* (here by the wood), not by
the wood insofar as it is wood, but by *the* wood *of which* the table is *made*.
The fundamental experience on the basis of which Plato determines the
ὄν as εἶδος, the experience of the ὄντως ὄν, is that of pure presence, the
character of which is to show itself.

The fundamental experience of Aristotle is determined in relation to
that of Plato. The prevailing interpretation is to claim that Plato restricts
reality to the Ideas above, and that Aristotle brings them back to earth
and, as it were, admits them into things: idealism and realism. Now
what is different here is that the εἶδος becomes the μορφή of a τόδε τι
in motion and rest. Aristotle grasps things as κινούμενα, and not as μὴ
ὄντα, and thus grasps them against the background of the experience of
κίνησις. See *Physics* Γ 201a 10-11: ἡ τοῦ δυνάμει ὄντος ἐντελέχεια, ἡ
τοιοῦτον, κίνησίς ἐστιν.

Because the κίνησίς is itself defined as ἐνέργεια (or rather ἐντελέχεια),
ἐνέργεια appears in Aristotle as the highest determination of being
itself.

September 6

After reading the protocol of the September 5 session, Heidegger recalls that the Latin translation of ἐνέργεια by *actus* prepared the interpretation of making as *"creatio,"* the source of which is, of course, the
creation story.

The actual session begins with the thought that all metaphysics rests
upon a fundamental experience of being, each time specific to a thinker:
for example, with Kant the fundamental experience is that of being as
"Nature." Experience—the key word of the *Critique of Pure Reason*—
does not have the vague sense of what is felt. Experience for Kant is
experience in the scientific sense, that is, in the sense of the science par
excellence which, since the beginning of modern times until today, is
mathematical physics. The determinative character of mathematical
physics within modern science in general shows itself today, for example, in the fact that biology becomes a biophysics, and that it is only as
biophysics that contemporary biology is able to predict and prepare the
mastery of the γένεσις of man. In the social sciences, we see the same
transformation: anthropology becomes an anthropo-physics, in which the
mathematical-statistical treatment of data constitutes the essential method.
More generally, we are to observe the appearance of cybernetics at the
cross-roads of contemporary science. We need to bear this in mind if we
want to understand the text of Hegel that we have before us in its
authentic dimension and not as a mere object of erudition.

The fundamental experience of the being of beings for any philosophical thinking determines what being will count as the standard. The being that is "Nature" for Kant, this being is "Spirit" for Hegel, spirit in the sense of absolute consciousness. We recall in this respect that it is with Descartes that philosophy, according to the very words of Hegel, reached for the first time the *terra firma* [*feste Land*] of "consciousness." The difference between Descartes and Hegel is that Descartes only sets foot on this land while Hegel thoroughly traverses it. Descartes discovers this land in the *Meditationes de prima philosophia*, Hegel measures it all throughout the entire *System of Logic*, that is to say, as much in *The Phenomenology of Spirit* as in the three parts of the *Logic*: logic of being, logic of essence as truth of being, and logic of the concept as truth of essence, in which being is included. In this surveying of the land, in this Hegelian geo-metry which measures out the land of consciousness in its totality, we are not speaking of a mathematical measure; the measure is metaphysical and total, that is to say, "absolute."

One definitively leaves this mathematical image as soon as one asks which method determines the absolute measure of the land of consciousness. This method is dialectic, which is accomplished in the faculty of Reason. It is in *The Difference Between Fichte's and Schelling's System of Philosophy* that there first emerges what will be Hegel's sole task: to determine the relation of reason to the absolute. We read here the following sentence (p. 35/114):

> The method of the system should be called neither synthetic nor analytic. It shows itself at its purest, when it appears as a development of Reason itself. Reason does not recall its appearance, which emanates from it as a duplicate, back into itself—for then, it would only nullify it. Rather, Reason constructs itself in its emanation as an identity that is conditioned by this very duplicate; it opposes this relative identity to itself once more, and in this way the system advances until the objective totality is completed. Reason then unites this objective totality with the opposite subjective totality to form the infinite world-intuition [*unendliche Weltanschauung*], whose expansion has at the same time contracted into the richest and simplest identity.

We begin the explication of this proposition (Heidegger notes that the goal of the seminar is to read all Hegelian texts on the basis of an understanding of this fundamental proposition) by the explication of the central expression: infinite world-intuition.

—What does "world" mean in "world-intuition"? World means, as already in the Kantian antinomies, being in its totality.

—What does "intuition" [*Anschauung*] mean? Also starting from the Kantian vocabulary, which must be done with Hegel as with Fichte and Schelling, intuition must be understood as the representation of the individual as individual, in opposition to the concept which, for its part, is the representation of something in general.

—What does "world-intuition" now mean? World-intuition means: the intuition of being in its totality, and since it is a matter of intuition, this totality is something individual, unique.

—Now, what does "infinite world-intuition" mean? What does "infinite intuition" mean? The finite is characterized in Hegel by fixity. To fix is to posit, in the sense of positing something apart, and consequently to posit it in an opposition. The position individuates something posited *against* something else. Thus for finitude, all determination, everything determined, is circumscribed by non-determination, by nothingness. *Omnis determinatio negatio est.* If this is the finite, the infinite is then that position which, on the contrary, does not let the opposites disappear, but preserves them in their opposition within their "conjoining."

To the extent that this conjoining, for its part, is also posited, it comes into opposition with another unity, and these two unities demand anew their own conjoining: such is the fundamental and internal law of dialectic.

The question that immediately assumes importance here is that of experiencing whether and how the dialectical movement itself is able to avoid falling back under the domination of the finite, in the guise of the bad infinite, of end-lessness. Several answers, in particular that of circularity, run into this difficulty without resolving it. It is just as futile to externally call upon the inalterability of the Absolute. It is also pointless to look for some point at which the bad infinite, as if by chance, would come to a halt. Let us look instead for an identity that would escape this difficulty in advance: it is the identity that Hegel calls in his text, "the most non-dichotomous identity" (34/113; tm).

Why is it said to be "most non-dichotomous"? Because this unity is precisely the one that does not originally know the *dichotomy*. Non-dichotomous is more precise than in-finite. Non-dichotomous names the two terms of the fixed opposition *at the same time,* in order to forestall them (their fixed dichotomy). What is thus expressed is a "positing" which is no longer the simple opposition of the opposites, nor the simple unity itself posited of opposites, in opposition to which another opposition arises which itself demands a new unity, but a unity such that it contains in itself all oppositions. This is, in the final analysis, the sense of the central speculative expression: "infinite world-intuition."

If, on the basis of this now clarified sentence, we turn to the sentence on page 14/91 ("When the power of conjoining, etc."), the richness and precision of what it says finally appears to us.

Thus, the Absolute is "the most non-dichotomous identity." If the theme of philosophy is to be the Absolute and dialectic its movement, the Absolute must therefore be seen at every step of the dialectic, but as not-yet unfolded. The task of reason is nothing other than its unfolding, that is, the binding of all opposites in the light of the most indivisible Identity, which is no longer in any way a relative identity. This is why Hegel writes somewhere that the sole interest of reason is to "sublate" the fixed opposites.

The last part of the session is devoted to the explication of the term "sublation" [*Aufheben*]. Sublation means:

1) "To place something on," for instance to place a book on the table in order to see it. The fundamental act of dialectic is indeed to first let the opposites come forth, in order to see them. "Sublation" in this first sense would be equivalent to the Latin "*tollere*," in the ordinary sense of taking ("*tolle, lege*").[56]

2) If the opposition of the two opposites is thus taken into view, sublation means: elevating them to their unity. This unity is like an arc which reaches higher than the two opposites facing each other, and to that extent sublation would be equivalent to the Latin "*elevare*."

3) Sublation means preserving, conserving, bringing to a safe place (for example, "to keep a gift well-preserved [*ein Geschenk gut aufheben*]"). This preservation is accomplished in the absolute identity where the opposites are conserved, instead of disappearing as the cows do in the night of Schellingian identity.

Jean Beaufret then notes that none of these three senses which are always present together in "sublation" have the slightest negative character, and that therefore to translate "*Aufhebung*" simply as "*suppression*" (suppression) or "*abolition*" (abolishment) is quite often absurd. The historic reach of this observation appears with respect to the well-known phrase from Kant: "I have therefore found it necessary to deny [*aufheben*] *knowledge*, in order to make room for *faith*."[57] This does not mean: to "abolish" knowledge, but indeed to first properly establish it, in that it is raised to its unity (possibility of experience), in its limits (or better, in its place), which is the authentic meaning of the critical delimitation and which must be understood positively. It is precisely this bringing-to-its-place of theoretical knowledge that allows the corresponding location of practical reason to become visible.

September 8

This session is the last. Heidegger observes that the seminar did not go as far as he had wished to take it. This, however, is neither a regret nor a reproach to anyone. The goal was to bring it to where the two fundamental terms of the opposition would emerge in their determinateness. These separate the fundamental experience of metaphysics from the question concerning the meaning of being, as it is first unfolded in *Being and Time*.

After this remark, we again take up the headings under which Hegel expresses the way Reason grasps the Absolute. These headings are: Reflection–Construction–Production–Contraction. The first question posed concerns the domain in which all of these moments of the grasping of the Absolute by Reason are accomplished. This domain is "consciousness."

1. First moment: Reflection. How does Hegel understand "reflection"? In order to answer, we return to the sentence from page 17/94: "The Absolute is to be reflected. . . ." Let us pay attention to Hegel's language, which does not say: "We must reflect *on* the Absolute," but "the Absolute is to be reflected." "To reflect something" is different from "to reflect on something." For example, I can reflect on this book, either on its binding, or also on the difficulty of reading it, etc. . . . Each time, the book appears "in a certain regard"—from a certain point of view. To "reflecting-on" there belongs a precisely determined horizon, the horizon *in which* I reflect on the book. Now, by itself, what does "to reflect" mean? There is no longer a perspective in which I grasp the matter in advance, there is no longer a determinate anticipation [*Vor-griff*]. "The Absolute is to be reflected," this is said outside of any "perspective." Any perspective in which the Absolute is grasped indeed misses the Absolute, because any perspective as such is finite. On the contrary, the Absolute is "the most non-dichotomous identity," that is, the unity that is the ultimate ground of all possible oppositions. That it must be reflected thus means that it must be reflected on the basis of itself, from out of the most simple and most accomplished unity. It means further that it should show itself to consciousness, that is, that it should reflect (mirror) itself for it. To mirror [*Sich spiegeln*], applied to the Absolute, says that "it brings itself to appearance." This type of "mirroring" entitles one to name this conception of Reason "speculative." With Leibniz (raised in this context by one of the participants), it is quite different: for him it is human Reason that is a mirror.

Thus the Absolute appears to Reason, to consciousness—this is the meaning of "being reflected" for the Absolute. However, how does Reason "capture" [*auffängt*] the phenomenon of the Absolute (since it does not receive [*empfängt*] it, for here there is no "receptivity")? In what way does Reason let the Absolute appear for itself? What is the relation of Reason to unity, that is to say, to being? The fundamental character of idealism in its relation to being is "positing," the *"positio."*

Now, what does "positing" [*Setzen*] mean? *"Ich setze einen Baum,"* this means "I am planting a tree." Even if that tree then later unfolds its growth from itself, it is, nevertheless, still I who first planted it. Can the Absolute be planted like a tree? Of course not, because it is *already* "posited," because it is "given," it is what I find as already-presencing there. Then, what does "positing" mean in characterizing the grasping of the Absolute?

That the Absolute appear for consciousness does not mean that the absolute would burst into consciousness as into a cage. It appears to consciousness already in relation to the fundamental character of consciousness: with "positing." The question returns: what sort of positing? This is an important question first for the interpretation of *Greek* thought. In Greek, positing is said θέσις, and appears in ἀπόθηκη, whose meaning is the same as ἀπόφανσις: to let a matter stand here from itself, as it is, i.e., presences. But the modern "positing" is different; the Latin *repraesentatio* is the best interpretation of it. "*Re-*" for the Moderns (*Re-praesentatio*) refers back to the *ego cogito. Re-* is here "back to me." The "I" lets something stand before it, which also means that this something has become an "object." All this, clear as it is, is nonetheless covered over by the presumptions of idealism.

The question of "representation," thus taken up, is now the occasion for a sort of exercise in "phenomenological kindergarten," where everything all of a sudden becomes too difficult because too simple, and where everyone finds themselves extremely "clumsy." This was a long and useful course of work, the steps of which were the following:

— *Repraesentatio*, that is, representation [*Vorstellung*]. For instance: The Louvre in Paris. For us right now it is a "representation." Where is it? In our heads? How can we then avoid saying, even more scientifically: in our brains? The autopsy of the brain does not reveal any "representations."

— It is then said that it concerns an image. The question thus arises: when we represent the Louvre to ourselves, is it an image that we make present to ourselves? No, it is rather the Louvre itself. *Always*, and even in the "making present," even when we relate to something simply in thought, I am in relation with the things themselves, as I am now in relation with this book here that I look at and with which I am concerned. However, despite this immediacy there are differences, and phenomenology must investigate their character. Although the Louvre is now not an image for me, I still cannot enter it through the door, while I can open the book which is here on this table. To the extent that the book is present-at-hand, we must therefore say that it presents [*vorstellt*] itself to me. "Representation" here means: the book itself "places itself before me." In opposition to a "making present," the relation here is that of a "perceiving."

What is characteristic of perception? A participant says, αἴσθησις, and is then told that "with the Greeks, and precisely in the distinction between αἴσθησις and νόησις, hell has already begun." What is important is the notion of "corporeality" [*Leibhaftigkeit*]: in perception what presences is "bodily" [*leibhaftig*]. This answer is in turn another question: what is that "body" from which the adjective "bodily" is formed? The French translation says, "*la chair*," the flesh. But flesh, the body as flesh, is what I myself am, it is my body [*Körper*], my lived-body [*Leib*]. Do I somehow extend my lived-body (as flesh) to the Louvre? No, and this is precisely why the Louvre is only the mere object of a simple "making present" (which, incidentally, nevertheless always includes the possibility of bodily perception, although not accomplished). It is therefore the lived-body that utterly characterizes perception. This lived-body is something like the reach of the human body (last night, the moon was closer than the Louvre).

—The word "body" that just appeared could jeopardize everything. We need to grasp the difference between "lived-body" and "body." For instance, when we step on a scale, we do not weigh our "lived-body" but merely the weight of our "body." Or further, the limit of the "lived-body" is not the limit of the "body." The limit of the body is the skin. The limit of the "lived-body" is more difficult to determine. It is not "world," but it is perhaps just as little "environment."

There is only "world" where there is language, that is, understanding of being. From this followed a few reflections on the work of Karl von Frisch, who attempted to determine what the bee *sees*. What "seeing" here means is in question, if one admits, despite a well-established French tradition, that cows never see trains pass by.[58]

Everyone then observes that we have taken a certain distance from Hegel, but Heidegger recalls that "phenomenological exercise is more important than reading Hegel," which does not in any way prevent us from returning to Hegel and from recapturing what has been said until now.

a) The Absolute is supposed to appear for humans—for consciousness.

b) The fundamental character of human consciousness for the Moderns is that of a "positing."

c) "Positing" (or *positio*) has several meanings. In contrast with "positing" in the sense of "planting a tree," there is θέσις in the sense of "to have *standing* before oneself."

From this we can understand the second moment of the grasp of the absolute by Reason: "Construction."

2. The Absolute must be "constructed" for consciousness. This construction is also termed "production." Let us precisely attend to these two terms.

When Marx says, "Man produces himself, etc. . . . ,"[59] it means: "Man is a factory. Man produces himself as he produces his shoes." But what does "Production" mean for Hegel? By no means that man produces the Absolute. Production is the figure of reflection's accomplishment.

In letting-appear, the Absolute is brought forth before consciousness, set alongside, that is, pro-duced. It is not a matter of a making, but rather of a "letting appear."

Construction, for its part, refers to architecture. The reason that represents the absolute (representing in the sense of bringing forth) is a reason that constructs (in the sense of architecture). This thought goes back to Kant: Reason is "knowledge derived from principles" and, by nature, "architectonic."[60] This means: it considers all knowledge as belonging to a possible system.

To summarize: Reason "reflects" the Absolute. This reflecting is a bringing-before-itself, that is, a pro-duction. This pro-duction is a construction, whereby construction means: belonging together in the self-showing of the Absolute as a belonging together that builds together (a setting together).[61]

3. Final Moment: "Contraction." This is now very easy to understand. *Cum-trahere*, this is drawing-together. Contraction is the "drawing together" of all the opposites to the highest unity of the Absolute.

Through these connected determinations we now have a clarification of the reflection of Reason, which is the object of page 17/94. We reread the first paragraph of the section entitled "Reflection as Instrument of Philosophizing" until "this task involves a contradiction" and especially emphasize these last words.[62] Reason contradicts itself; it forbids itself what it wants. The origin of this "contradiction" is that "all production has the character of θέσις, of σύνθεσις; thus the entire activity of Reason, as a positing, is something limited." This is why Hegel cautiously says: the Absolute *is to be* reflected.[63]

This contradiction must be resolved, otherwise the Absolute would not be "posited" but sublated. At this point on page 17/94, "sublation" does not have the positive sense that we just acknowledged concerning the characteristic feature of Hegelian dialectic. "Sublated" means here (page 17/94), if not that the Absolute would be "suppressed in appearing," at least that access would not be conceded.

The end of the paragraph warrants particular attention, due to the introduction of the "non-conscious" [*das Bewußtlose*].[64] The non-conscious immediately evokes Freud. But the difference is extreme, and not only because Freud says "the unconscious" [*das Unbewußte*] and not the "non-conscious." The difference is that the Freudian "unconscious" does not belong "in consciousness" while for Hegel the difference between the "conscious" and the "non-conscious" does belong to consciousness: ". . . *constructed in consciousness* as the Absolute that is both conscious and non-conscious. . . ." If the characteristic feature of consciousness for modern thinkers is "positing," then it must be understood that "as conscious" means in this sentence "as posited," and that consequently "as non-conscious" means as "not yet posited, not yet sublated." Generally, Hegel's language is always to be understood as speculative language, and not as "normal" language.

What is a speculative statement? How is it different from an ordinary statement? Heidegger takes as an example the statement: *Deus est ipsum esse:* God is being itself. This is a *normal* metaphysical statement, not a speculative one (contrary to what its "lofty" theme might suggest). We reach the speculative when the predicate of this sentence (being) is made into a subject, becomes subject. Namely: being is God. This is no mere reversal of the grammatical structure of the normal sentence. It has changed something, and, indeed, it is the meaning of "is" that has changed. The simple reversal would mean: being is God, like the simple reversal of "the rose is a plant" would yield "the plant is a rose." Yet it is not merely a reversal but a *counter-blow,* a counter movement of the second "is" upon the first "is." Now, what does "is" mean when overturned in this manner? Meister Eckhart said: *Istic-heit.* Being is God, now understood speculatively, means: Being *"istet"* God, that is, Being lets God be God. "Is" speaks here in the transitive and the active. The unfolded Being itself (as it is unfolded in Hegel's *Logic*) first makes possible (in a speculative recoil) being-God.

The session ends on the silence created by the wind of speculation.

September 2

The text serving as a basis for the work is Kant's "The Sole Possible Proof for a Demonstration of the Existence of God" (1763), more precisely, the "First Observation: Of Existence As a Whole."

This seminar aims to elucidate Kant's text *indirectly*. Indeed, one must keep in view that Kant himself altered his interpretation of being twenty years later.

The path our mediate elucidation will take is the question of being, the question concerning being, along with how it has unfolded from *Being and Time* to today.

So we pose the question: what does the "question of being" mean? For, as a question, the question of being already offers numerous possibilities for misunderstanding—something confirmed by the continual failure to understand the book *Being and Time*.

What does "the question of being" mean? One says "being" and from the outset one understands the word metaphysically, i.e., from out of metaphysics. However, in metaphysics and its tradition, "being" means: that which determines a being insofar as it is a being. As a result, metaphysically the question of being means: the question concerning the being *as* a being, or otherwise put: the question concerning the ground of a being.

To this question, the history of metaphysics has given a series of answers. As an example: ἐνέργεια. Here reference is made to the Aristotelian answer to the question "What is the being as a being?"—an answer which runs ἐνέργεια, and not some ὑποκείμενον. For its part, the ὑποκείμενον is an interpretation of beings and by no means an interpretation of being. In the most concrete terms, ὑποκείμενον is the presencing of an island or of a mountain, and when one is in Greece such a presencing leaps into view. Ὑποκείμενον is in fact the being as it lets itself be seen, and this means: that which is there before the eyes, as it brings itself forth from itself. Thus the mountain lies on land and the island in the sea.

Such is the Greek experience of beings.

For us, being as a whole—τὰ ὄντα—is only an empty word. For us, there is no longer that experience of beings in the Greek sense. On the contrary, as in Wittgenstein: "The real is what is the case"[65] (which means: that which falls under a determination, lets itself be established, the determinable), actually an eerie statement.

For the Greeks, on the contrary, this experience of beings is so rich, so concrete and *touches* the Greeks to such an extent that there are significant synonyms (Aristotle, *Metaphysics* A): τὰ φαινόμενα, τὰ ἀληθέα. For this reason, it gets us nowhere to translate τὰ ὄντα literally as "the beings." In so doing, there is no understanding of what is being for the Greeks. It is authentically: τὰ ἀληθέα, what is revealed in uncon-cealment, what postpones concealment for a time; it is τὰ φαινόμενα, what here shows itself from itself.

A supplementary question regarding the ὑποκείμενον is then posed. How is the experience of a being different when it is understood as ὑποκείμενον from when it is understood as φαινόμενον? Suppose we look upon a particular being, for example a mountain in the Lubéron.[66] If it is taken as ὑποκείμενον, then the ὑπο names a κατά, more precisely the κατά of a λέγειν τι κατὰ τινός. Of course, the Lubéron mountain does not actually disappear if it is spoken of as a ὑποκείμενον, but it no longer stands there as a *phenomenon* — no longer to be seen here as giving itself from itself. It no longer presences itself from itself. As ὑποκείμενον it is *that about which* we speak. Here it is crucial to make a fundamental distinction in regard to speaking, namely by distinguishing pure nomi-nation (ὀνομάζειν) from the making of a proposition (λέγειν τι κατὰ τινός).

In simple nomination, I let what is present be what it is. Without a doubt naming includes the one who names — but what is proper to nam-ing is precisely that the one who names intervenes only to step into the background before the being. The being then is pure phenomenon.

With a proposition, on the contrary, the one making the proposition takes part. He inserts himself into it — and he inserts himself into it as the one who ranges over the being in order to speak *about* it. As soon as that occurs, the being can now only be understood as ὑποκείμενον and the name only as a residue of the ἀπόφανσις.

Today, when all language is from the outset understood as proposi-tion, it is very difficult for us to experience naming as pure nomination, outside of all κατάφασις and in such a way that it lets the being pres-ence as pure phenomenon.

But what is "phenomenon" in the Greek sense? According to the modern way of speaking, "phenomenon" for the Greeks is precisely what cannot become a phenomenon for modernity; it is the thing itself, the thing in itself. Between Aristotle and Kant there lies an abyss. Here one must guard oneself against any retrospective interpretation. And thus the decisive question must be posed: in what way are τὰ ὄντα and τὰ φαινόμενα synonymous for the Greeks? Just how are what pres-ences and what shows itself from itself (what appears) united? For Kant, such a unity is simply impossible.

For the Greeks, things appear.

For Kant, things appear to me.

In the time between them, it has come about that the being has become an ob-ject (*obiectum*, or better yet: *res obstans*). The expression "object" simply has no correlate in Greek.

For Hegel, Greek philosophy is interpreted as "merely objective," which the Modern and Hegelian interpretations present as what Greek philosophy truly was. What Hegel thereby actually says is that the Greeks had not yet thought the subjective as mediation and hence as the core of objectivity. In this manner, while Hegel says something that in one way corresponds to Greek philosophy, he nonetheless obstructs access to the Greek meaning of being from the ground up. This is the case because the Hegelian interpretation tacitly suggests that Greek philosophy had not thought dialectical mediation, i.e., had not thought consciousness as the key to the becoming-phenomena of the phenomena. If he thinks in this way, and he does so think, then Hegel ultimately excludes himself from the Greek experience of a being as phenomenon.

He further says that the Greeks did experience the immediate, but for him that means something negative, a poverty of those who begin, for whom the experience of dialectical mediation is still lacking.

What has occurred between the Greeks and Hegel?

The thinking of Descartes. Hegel says that with him, thinking reaches "terra firma" for the first time. What Descartes undertakes is actually to determine ground by *firmness*—therefore to no longer let a ground be as it is from itself. In reality, Descartes surrenders the ground. He abandons it for the sake of firmness. What sort of firmness is this? Where does the firmness of the *firmum* come from for Descartes? He says it himself: from *punctum firmum et inconcussum.*[67] *Inconcussum*, i.e., unshakable, namely unshakable for knowledge, for consciousness, for *perceptio* (with Descartes knowledge becomes *perceptio*). The human is henceforth placed into his position as *representer*.

As we come back to the phenomena from here, the question arises: how are the φαινόμενα possible? Answer: by ἀλήθεια. The Greeks are those human beings who lived immediately in the openness of phenomena—through the expressly ek-static capacity of letting the phenomena speak to them (modern man, Cartesian man, *se solum alloquendo*, only talks to himself).

No one has ever again reached the heights of the Greek experience of a being as phenomenon. To gain an intimation of this, one need only consider the fact that there is no Greek word by which to say the being of the human in ἀλήθεια. There is nothing close. Not even in Greek poetry, where the being of the human is nonetheless brought to its pinnacle. Consequently, to name this being *"existing"* . . . the word has become so common, that it is open to every misunderstanding. If there is no Greek word for this ek-static existence, it is not so due to a lack, but rather an excess. The Greeks belong in their being to ἀλήθεια, in which the being unveils itself in its phenomenality. Accordingly this is their destiny: Μοῖρα.

Placing ourselves before the equivalence of meaning between *a being* and *phenomenon*, we ask: how does philosophy arise from the Greek residence in the midst of phenomena? To what extent is philosophy only able, and was only able, to emerge among the Greeks? From where does philosophy receive its first impetus, which sets it upon its way? Succinctly put, what is the beginning of philosophy? These questions lead back to a main question: In the relationship of Greek humanity to beings, in the sense of what is unconcealed, is there something that makes philosophy (as investigation into the being of beings) necessary?

However difficult it may be for us to accomplish anew what the Greeks did when they thought the being as an appearing outside of concealment, as coming-forth-out-of-concealment (in the sense of φύσις), we nevertheless ask: what occurs in the fact of arising-into-ἀλήθεια? What is at once co-named in the word φύειν?

It is the *overabundance*, the *excess* of what presences. Here one should recall the anecdote of Thales: he is that person so struck by the over-abundance of the world of stars that he was compelled to direct his gaze towards the heavens *alone*. In the Greek climate,[68] the human is so overwhelmed by the presencing of what presences, that he is compelled to the question concerning what presences *as* what presences. The Greeks name the relation to this thrust of presence θαυμάζειν.[69]

In extreme opposition to this, one can say that when the astronauts set foot on the moon, the moon *as* moon disappeared. It no longer rose or set. It is now only a calculable parameter for the technological enterprise of humans.

Clearly, what is decisive in all this is that the privation, the α of ἀλήθεια, corresponds to this excess. Privation is not negation. The more strongly it becomes what the word φύειν indicates, the more powerful is the source from which it springs, the concealment in unconcealment.

Consequently, it must always be emphasized that the dimension of the entirely excessive is that in which philosophy arises. Philosophy is indeed the answer of a humanity that has been struck by the excess of presence—an answer which is itself excessive, and one which leads to a more precise formulation: that philosophy as philosophy is no Greek way of ek-sisting, but rather a *hyper-Greek* way [*eine übergriechische Weise des Ek-sistierens ist*]. With this, we can understand the second part of the anecdote concerning Thales, who is so struck by what he sees that he no longer attends to the common things before his feet and falls into a well. To summarize: the Greeks are involved with ἀλήθεια in that they are usually occupied *within* ἀλήθεια. But it is *with* ἀλήθεια that the philosophers, those who are more Greek than the Greeks, are concerned, though admittedly not coming so far as to pose the *question of* ἀλήθεια (as such).

So the question is posed: in which form and to what extent is ἀλήθεια visible to the Greeks? Answer: in the form of τὸ αὐτό of νοεῖν and εἶναι, as expressed in the poem of Parmenides.

This answer leads to the question concerning the Greek sense of *knowing*. In Greek, knowledge is named νοεῖν and ἰδεῖν—as both indicate being open for that which gives itself from itself. The correspondence of the Parmenidean τὸ αὐτό with the λόγος of Heraclitus is to be understood from this: both name that gathering in which being makes its address.

And so the answer must run: for the Greeks ἀλήθεια is visible as λόγος, and λόγος means, much more originally than "to speak": *to let* presencing [*Anwesen* lassen].

We took as our point of departure the question: what does "the question of being" mean? Because one understands it metaphysically as the question concerning the being of beings—and *the former* question has even led to this—the question concerning being *as being* has never been posed.

We will attempt to confirm this by investigating one of the most prominent answers to the metaphysical question concerning the being of beings: that of Plato.

The εἶδος is the being of beings, just as, in its Cartesian sense, the *idea* is such for the modern era. What is this εἶδος as first answer to the Greek question: What is the being of beings? How is this answer to be understood from what we have considered up to now?

That the being of *this* book should be an "idea," that is straight away incomprehensible! For Plato, this book is a μὴ ὄν. Nevertheless, it is no οὐκ ὄν, no nothing, no non-being, for it is there. But it is not a being, insofar as it is *not that* which lets it be as this being that it is.

This book is only a particular way of making the book-essence [*das Buch-Wesen*] perceptible. The οὐκ ὄν must here be distinguished from the μὴ ὄν, negation distinguished from privation. Privation expresses itself through a lack, and this lack breaks out in the difference between εἶδος and εἴδωλον. This particular book is not εἶδος, but rather εἴδωλον.

Certainly there are many books which are not *this particular* book and are nevertheless still books. What is the pure essence of the book? In what sense can it be said that the εἶδος is the ὄντως ὄν? Where is this most extreme excess in the case of this book here? How does the Platonic idea precisely correspond to what the Greeks named presence, οὐσία?

To be subject to change, to alter oneself, this is to take distance from something previous: to absence. The idea alone is pure presence, presence never absencing, a self-maintaining-making-present. This is what is there in excess: the presencing presence [*anwesende Anwesenheit*] — such is the ὄντως ὄν. Nietzsche had the strongest sense for this, especially in the text: "How the 'true world' finally became a fable" (*Twilight of the Idols*).[70]

It is then to be remarked that "the being" for Plato must be understood much more in the verbal sense: being [*das Seiend*], than in the nominal sense: the being [*das Seiende*].

We must never allow ourselves to lose sight of the fact that the determinations of φαίνεσθαι and of the ἀληθές are fully presented in the Platonic εἶδος. One is ever tempted to hear ἰδεῖν in ἰδέα, whereas what is primary is the appearance [*Aussehen*], the way and manner by which the thing is characterized, and not the view that one has of it, a view that one is only able to form on the basis of what the appearance first *puts forth*. Nothing is less Greek than what Schopenhauer says of Plato (meant is the statement about the desert that exists only thanks to my thinking of it); contrary to Schopenhauer, Aristotle says: Even if no man were to see them, the stars for that reason would shine nonetheless.[71]

What is said of the question of being in *Being and Time?* In *Being and Time*, the question, "What is a being?" is not asked, but rather, What is this "is"?

Immediately one runs into a difficulty. In fact, if the "is" *is*, then it is a being! And if, on the other hand, it *is* not, then is it supposed to be the bare, empty copula of a judgment?

One must come out of this aporia. From a purely grammatical point of view, "to be" is not only a verb, it is a helping verb. If, however, one thinks beyond the grammatical, one must ask: is *to be*, as an infinitive, only an abstraction derived from "is" — or is one only able to say "is" if *being* is already opened up and manifest?

For this reason, *Being and Time* addresses this question from the perspective of the *meaning* of Being.

Meaning has a very precise signification in *Being and Time*, even if today it has become insufficient. What does "meaning of being" mean? This is understandable on the basis of the "project region" unfolded by the "understanding of being." "Understanding" [*Verständnis*], for its part, must be grasped in the original sense of "standing before" [*Vorstehen*]: residing before, holding oneself at an equal height with what one finds before oneself, and being strong enough to hold out.[72]

Here "meaning" is to be understood from "project," which is explained by "understanding."

What is inappropriate in this formulation of the question is that it makes it all too possible to understand the "project" as a human performance. Accordingly, project is then only taken to be a structure of subjectivity—which is how Sartre takes it, by basing himself upon Descartes (for whom ἀλήθεια as ἀλήθεια does not arise).

In order to counter this mistaken conception and to retain the meaning of "project" as it is to be taken (that of the opening disclosure), the thinking after *Being and Time* replaced the expression "meaning of being" with "truth of being." And, in order to avoid any falsification of the sense of truth, in order to exclude its being understood as correctness, "truth of being" was explained by "location of being" [*Ortschaft*] — truth as locality [*Örtlichkeit*] of being. This already presupposes, however, an understanding of the place-being of place. Hence the expression *topology of be-ing* [Topologie des Seyns], which, for example, one finds in *Aus der Erfahrung des Denkens;* also see the text edited by Franz Larese: "*Die Kunst und der Raum.*"[73]

September 4

Some additions were first made to the protocol of September 2.

We have moved away too quickly from the distinction between ὑποκείμενον and φαινόμενον. At that opportunity we did not sufficiently emphasize what it is that both are in relation to, despite their differences from one another:

a) The φαινόμενον actually bears a relation to and always presupposes as its horizon ἀλήθεια, an ἀλήθεια, however, constantly understood already and in advance from λέγειν (as indeed by Homer; on this see "Hegel and the Greeks"[74]). This first and decisive understanding of ἀλήθεια as the ἀλήθεια of the λόγος barred the Greeks from the possibility of thinking ἀλήθεια as ἀ-λήθεια (as unconcealment); that is, as clearing [*Lichtung*]. Important here is that only the thought of the clearing of being is able to bring the necessary clarity to make the λόγος itself understandable.

b) The ὑποκείμενον is the being (therefore the φαινόμενον), but only insofar as it is explicitly viewed within a λέγειν τι κατὰ τινός (a "saying something about something"). It is then remarked that, in a certain way, the Aristotelian investigation of language accomplishes the most original interpretation of language, one that was already dominant in the poetry of Homer (as *epic* poetry). In Greek, naming always already and in advance signifies *making a proposition* [*Aussagen*], and to make a proposition means to make something known *as* something. This understanding of language predetermines the region in which Homeric poetry moves (on this, consider the breadth of a word from Mallarmé: "Since the great Homeric errancy, poetry has entirely strayed from its course"[75]).

Heidegger then emphasizes that for Hölderlin, on the contrary, to name means to call, and in this way the thoroughly unpoetic nature of the Greek interpretation of language is established. And, nevertheless, there is no higher poetry than that in Greece!

One thing is nevertheless certain: the conception of saying as the making of a proposition obstructs access to an understanding of the essence of poetry. As testament to this, it suffices to read Aristotle's *Poetics*.

The second point: we go once more into the distinction between εἶδος and εἴδωολον and note that the essence of the lack that presences in the εἴδωολον is to alter the presence of the εἶδος. For Plato, the wood out of which a cane is produced is more an obscuring of the εἶδος than a bearer of it. This becomes visible, for example, when, suppressing the cane-εἶδος still further, I dip the cane in water: the cane then "breaks." One can then say for Plato that the wood of the cane breaks the cane-εἶδος; the result of this break is this particular cane here, a cane-image [*Abbild*]: μὴ ὄν. To conclude this addendum, it is mentioned that εἶδος becomes μορφή in Aristotle (the μορφή includes ποίησις); and that the ὕλη is the *from-which* for the μορφή (as is the wood for the cane-εἶδος). In this Aristotelian analysis of beings, one clearly sees an emphasis upon poietic terminology.

Resumption of the seminar:

The previous session concluded with a recollection upon how the question of being was first raised in *Being and Time*. Now Heidegger intends to present the process of thinking that led up to the emergence of that work.

He begins by naming the authentic name of the method followed: "destruction" — this must be understood in the strong sense as *de-struere*, "dis-mantling" ["*Ab-bauen*"], and not as devastation.

But what is dismantled? Answer: that which covers over the meaning of being, the structures amassed upon one another that make the meaning of being unrecognizable.

Further, destruction strives to free the original meaning of being. This original meaning is presence. This meaning governs all Greek understanding of being, without its knowing it. When Plato determines the ἰδέα as ὄντως ὄν, he establishes in a decisive way the being of beings as presencing presence [*anwesende Anwesenheit*].

In this determination of the meaning of being by presence, however, there is a *temporal* moment that lies concealed. The thinking that questions after the meaning of being is thus required to expressly pose the question of the relation between being AND time.

With this step, the question enters into a new difficulty: which time does it concern and how is this time to be thought? Now it is the case that in *Physics* IV Aristotle has written the fundamental treatise for all philosophical thinking of time. Can one relate the position of inquiry in

Being and Time to the Aristotelian investigation? No. Aristotle thinks time *in departure* from the Greek interpretation of being—which from the outset is founded upon a temporal determination (as presencing). Otherwise put, in regards to time Aristotle poses the question: what is time?—and in this way actually asks: what is extant [*seiend*] in time?— without regard for the circumstance that in this reduction, already from the start and surreptitiously, a temporal predetermination is operative.

All metaphysics up to Hegel persists in thinking time always in departure from the leading interpretation of the being of beings. So, for example, with Kant time is conceived in the horizon of ob-jectivity [Gegen-*ständ*lichkeit] as *that which holds itself steady* in the constant flow of the changing now.

In metaphysics, and first of all in Aristotle, there is thus a genuine short-circuiting of the meditation upon time from which there developed what *Being and Time* called the covering over of the meaning of being. Thinking must consequently attempt to further a new—non-metaphysical—way of thinking time, a way that is not surreptitiously governed by the ontological presupposition of the beinghood of time. The effect of this upon the metaphysical concept of time results in its being entirely concentrated upon what *presences* (actually only what presences *is;* and along with what presences, having-been and futurity are conditioned by a lack of being, they are consequences of μὴ ὄντα).

How is a non-metaphysical thinking of time possible? It is possible by way of an analysis of the temporality of Dasein. The essential character of this temporality rests in ek-stasis, which means in the fundamental resolution [*Erschlossenheit*] of Dasein for ἀλήθεια. In fact, ek-stasis is nothing other than the relation of Dasein to ἀλήθεια, in which all temporality arises.

Viewed in this manner, time is no longer a series of now-moments, but instead itself the horizon for the understanding of being. The analytic of Dasein, in effect, provides the equipment that makes possible a delimitation of the sense of being in its non-metaphysical signification. With this, destruction achieves its goal. But it is now clear that the various coverings of the originary sense of being maintain an essential relation to what they cover over. The history of metaphysics thus receives, from the ground up, another meaning. From now on, its various basic positions can be understood positively as transformations of the original meaning. Each time new, they follow upon one another, belonging together in the unity of a single destiny—hence the name destiny of being [*Seinsgeschick*] to indicate the epochs of being.

In the history of this concealment of being, which the history of metaphysics presents, thinking can pursue the history of being itself and consequently make a beginning with the next step along its path: the taking-into-view of being *as* being.

September 6

This morning Roger Munier arrived for the first time. Heidegger wished to take up the seven questions concerning technology that Munier had raised here on September 11, 1966.[76]

The seven questions read:

1) In *Gelassenheit* you speak of a "power concealed in modern technology."[77] What is this power that we still do not know how to name and that is "not made by man"?[78] Is it positive in its origin?

2) In regard to this power, you seem to admit that one needs to, if not belong to it, then at the very least correspond to it in a certain way, if one is to take up the new relationship that this power introduces between human and world.

In this context, what you say in "Hebel, the Friend of the House" is significant:

> We are errant today in a world which is a house without a friend, that is, which lacks that house-friend who in equal manner and with equal force is inclined toward both the technologically constructed world-edifice and the world as the house for a more original dwelling. Missing is that friend of the house who is able to re-entrust the calculability and technology of nature to the open mystery of a newly experienced naturalness of nature.[79]

What thinker can ever help us reconcile these two "realms" that have grown foreign to one another, and which "with a constant acceleration are racing even further apart": "the technologically dominable nature of science, and the natural nature of the . . . dwelling of man."[80]

In a word, who would be able to determine the conditions of a new rootedness?

3) "Releasement," the comportment of "self-joining" [*Sicheinfügens*], includes above all a cautious sheltering. It is an opening to the secret, to the unknown, which presents to us the technologically mastered world we are heading toward. Above all, it is a refusal to condemn this world. But there is still more to this. You explicitly say of this "other relationship to things" that the technological world which "demands of us the production and use of machines . . . is nevertheless not meaningless."[81] How do you understand this?

4) In other words, how is the significance of technological objects to be determined? Does this meaning go beyond simply serving to improve the conditions of our material lives and thus even beyond our liberation for greater tasks? Do they have a significance in themselves, and if so which?

5) If one only wished to consider the danger that is presented by its increasing expansion, could it not be said that this expansion itself, in its very excess, is the sort conducive to an attentiveness to the simple?

Will the rapid spreading of technological things not finally bring about an essential poverty, from which a turning around of the human to the truth of its essence becomes possible, even if by a detour of errancy?

6) Or are we to accept that a new dimension of the essence of the human is to be discovered on the basis of the human's experience of mastery over nature? The scientific interpretation of the world and of natural phenomena brings about a situation where everyday the human loses more and more of an already immemorial naturalness. But what harm does that do when it makes us attentive to what is indicated by these now and henceforth mastered world phenomena — when, as a result, other more original ways of expressing the secret are unfolded, something which the appearances attest to in their own way nonetheless? What significance are we to confer upon the new, unpoetic vision of the world in which we live?

7) In fact, everything advanced above rests on suppositions. We are not yet any further than when we first inquired into the meaning of this technological world, whose power grows daily. May we hope that this meaning will grow in clarity in harmony with the essence of the human, or must it remain of its own accord closed to us? How is that statement, according to which "the meaning of the technological world conceals itself,"[82] to be understood?

After the reading of these questions, Heidegger recalled that they were presented to him in writing three years ago and until now have remained unanswered.

The time passed since then sufficiently indicates the difficulty that they raise. It is not easy to answer these questions. Perhaps it amounted above all to preparing the right position of inquiry presupposed by these questions; otherwise said: to unfolding the question concerning technology.

Now it so happens that by a fortunate coincidence the work undertaken in the last two sessions at Le Thor was immersed in the theme of the text, "Kant's Thesis About Being,"[83] in which the interpretation of being that lays in an unrecognized manner at the bottom of all modern science and its technological character is investigated.

From the outset, then, we have a unified question where the modern interpretation of being as *position* converges with the totality of self-evident presuppositions and this convergence nourishes, as it were, modern technological thinking.

There is a text by Kant in which this unity expressly appears: the preface to the *Metaphysical Foundations of Natural Science*,[84] where the title already indicates the unity of the two regions.

This preface, Heidegger remarks in passing, would be an exceptional text for a seminar: the problem of movedness [*Bewegtheit*] is taken up there—a problem already central to Aristotle's *Physics*—but is no longer conceived by Kant in the table of categories, a noteworthy event and a sign of modernity. This amounts to saying that Kant did not unfold the relation of movedness to *being*.

One can thus see, in a towering example, the difficulty of thinking together, or even in their relation to one another, the question concerning technology and the question of being—questions which are nevertheless inextricably bound up with one another.

After the reading of the protocol from the last session, the actual seminar is resumed, with its elucidation of the expression "forgetfulness of being."

Usually one understands "to forget" in the sense of something falling away, as when one leaves an umbrella standing somewhere. Being is not forgotten in this sense.

"To forget" and "forgetfulness" must constantly be understood from Λήθη and ἐπιλανθάνεσθαι—which excludes any negative character.

As when, for example, Heraclitus says: φύσις κρύπτεσθαι φιλεῖ, "Self-concealment is the innermost essence of the movement of appearing." At this opportunity, a remark is made of the translation: φιλεῖ cannot be understood by "love" (when this is understood ontically as an occasional inclination). Φιλεῖ here means: "is essential for . . . to unfold its own being."

Hence, the fragment reads: "Emergence has as its accompanying necessity concealment." In the translation by Jean Beaufret: *Rien n'est plus propre à l'éclosion que le retrait*. Or better: *Rien n'est plus cher à l'éclosion que le retrait*.[85]

Such is the exceptional knowledge of φύσις by Heraclitus. But what does φύσις mean? What does this point to?

Much more than to *Natura*—in which, despite the manifest stress upon *nasci*, concealment is completely lacking—Φύσις points to ἀλήθεια itself. In this saying of Heraclitus, therefore, the thoroughly positive sense of "forgetfulness" still completely shines through. It becomes visible that being is not "subject to falling-out-of-attention," but rather *conceals itself* to the extent that it is manifest. After this was called to mind, the investigation of the "question of being" is again taken up.

According to the tradition, the "question of being" means the question concerning the being of beings, in other words: the question concerning the beinghood of beings, in which a being is determined in regard to its being-a-being [*Seiendsein*]. This question is *the* question of metaphysics.

With *Being and Time*, however, the "question of being" receives an entirely other meaning. Here it concerns the question of being as being. It becomes thematic in *Being and Time* under the name of the "question of the meaning [*Sinn*] of being."

Later this formulation was given up in favor of that of the "question concerning the truth of being," and finally in favor of that of the "question concerning the place or location of being," from which the name "topology of being" arose.

Three terms which succeed one another and at the same time indicate three steps along the way of thinking:

MEANING — TRUTH — PLACE (τόπος)

If the question of being is supposed to become clarified, what binds together the three successive formulations must necessarily be disclosed, along with what distinguishes them.

First, *truth.*

Let us observe that the expression "truth of being" has strictly no meaning when truth is understood as the correctness of a proposition. On the contrary, *truth* is here understood as "unconcealment," and more precisely still, taken from the perspective of Dasein, as clearing. Truth of being says clearing of being.

What then has happened in and through the alteration that lets *truth* take the place of *meaning*?

First, what does "meaning" signify? Meaning in *Being and Time* is defined in terms of a project region, and projection is the accomplishment of Dasein, which means the ek-static instancy [*Inständigkeit*] in the openness of being. By ek-sisting, Dasein includes *meaning.* The thinking that proceeds from *Being and Time,* in that it gives up the word "meaning of being" in favor of "truth of being," henceforth emphasizes the openness of being itself, rather than the openness of Dasein in regard to this openness of being.

This signifies "the turn," in which thinking always more decisively turns to being as being.

Now, what is the binding factor that unites *meaning* and *truth* (as unconcealment) and relates them to each other?

The ordinary sense of meaning is signification [*Bedeutung*]. As, for example, in the title from Franz von Brentano: *On the Manifold Meaning of Being in Aristotle.* Here meaning is understood as a bestowing of meaning, which means the conferring of a meaning. Husserl, too, treats of "sense-giving" acts in the chapter of the *Logical Investigations* entitled, "Expression and Meaning."[86]

Nevertheless, *Being and Time* does not undertake to present a new signification of being, but rather to open a hearing for the word of being — to let itself be claimed by being. In order to *be* the there [*Da*], it is a matter of becoming claimed by being.

But a question here announces itself: does being *speak?* And do we not already run the danger of degrading being into a being that speaks? But who decided that only a being can speak? Who has so gauged the essence of the word? Obviously these considerations lead directly to a new meditation on the word: *On the Way to Language.*

Indeed, in these remarks, one thing has come forth on its own: all our considerations take off from a fundamental distinction which can be expressed thusly: being is not a being.

This is the *ontological difference.*

How is this to be understood? Difference, διαφορά, means to keep separate. The ontological difference holds being and the being together at a distance from one another.

This difference would not be produced by metaphysics; instead it maintains and subtends metaphysics. Spoken in a Kantian manner, the ontological difference is the condition of possibility for ontology.

Why is the ontological difference not able to become a theme for metaphysics? Because if this were the case, the ontological difference would be a being and no longer the difference between being and beings. Hereby it becomes evident that the Diltheyan project of a metaphysics of metaphysics is impossible.

One can say in brief summary: the difference between being and beings reigns through all philosophy, fundamentally concealed and never thematized. But since the thinking of *Being and Time* sought to achieve the hearing of being as being, since accordingly the ontological difference becomes an explicit theme, is it not necessary to utter the strange statement, "being is not a being," which means, "being is nothing"?

The statement is estranging in the sense that it says of being that it "is," while indeed the being alone *is.* Difference stubbornly resists the attempt to say it *as* difference; and being likewise resists the attempt to say it *as* being.

Heidegger indicates that it is better here to give up the "is" — and to simply write:

being : nothing

Will someone not object, however, that these formulations, whose strange character we have just emphasized, in fact already arise in metaphysics? Does not Hegel say, for example at the beginning of the *Logic:* "Pure being and pure nothing are, therefore, the same"?[87] The task here is, first of all, to understand the statement correctly. Even more intently then: what relation could there be between being and nothing for Hegel and this formulation, to which the extra-metaphysical grounding of the ontological difference as concealed source of metaphysics has led? In order to situate this question, the seminar now asks about the *place* in Hegel's thinking where the above cited statement is to be found.

It stands at the beginning of the *Logic.* This title actually reads *Science of Logic* [*Wissenschaft der Logik*]. The expression speaks from out of the horizon of a knowledge [*Wissen*] (for which Hegel provides an image by saying that it concerns the thought of God before the creation).

This knowledge has a precise philosophical meaning. It is no knowledge in the sense that the science of nature is a knowledge. It is connected much more with that knowledge which Fichte made the center and knot of his thinking in the *Doctrine of Science* [*Wissenschaftslehre*] (1794).

It is that knowledge, which more originally than all objective knowledge, is a *self*-knowledge. With Fichte, the absolutizing of the Cartesian *cogito* (which is a *cogito* only insofar as it is completed as a *cogito me cogitare*) leads to ABSOLUTE KNOWLEDGE.

Absolute knowledge is the place of absolute certainty, in which absolute knowledge knows itself. Only in this way can "science," or the knowledge of knowledge, be understood—which now becomes an exact synonym for "philosophy."

The place where Hegel's proposition arises can thus be precisely determined: it is consciousness [*Bewußtsein*], the place of its own conscious being. The constitution of its own conscious being includes that there is only consciousness of an object insofar as consciousness, still more originally, is a being conscious of itself. More precisely, and here one recognizes the Kantian contribution to the Cartesian theme: anything certain arises from the mediation of self-certainty. Otherwise put: all knowledge of objectivity is beforehand a knowledge-about-oneself.

Now it can be understood in what sense being for Hegel is the indeterminate immediate. Across from consciousness, which is only consciousness of something insofar as it is first and originally a reflection of consciousness upon itself, being is the *antipode* [Entgegengesetzte] of consciousness. In respect to consciousness as mediation, it is the immediate. In respect to consciousness as determination, it is the indeterminate. Hence being is for Hegel the moment of the absolute alienation of the absolute. This is why the Nothing is the Same as being. It is to be understood that, starting from consciousness, the nothing is just as originarily grasped as being.

In the lecture "What is Metaphysics?"[88] the point of departure is from the outset a completely different one. The lecture does not actually speak of consciousness [*Bewußtseins*] being conscious of itself, but rather of Da-sein.

The last, most difficult step remains to be taken, for which, after more than two hours of work, the strength is beginning to wane: to ask about the difference between the experience of non-being [*Nichtseienden*], of the nothing, in "What is Metaphysics?" and in Hegel's statement.

The session concluded with a reference to the sentence "Why are there beings at all and not, far rather, nothing?" which is first spoken by

Leibniz, taken up a second time by Schelling, and a third time in the
lecture "What is Metaphysics?"

To reflect upon the three successive versions of this sentence means
to get underway towards a new understanding of being—with which,
no doubt, it would be possible to discuss in its full scope the question
concerning technology which opened this work session.

September 7

In Hegel's statement, "Pure being and pure nothing are, therefore, the
same," the same words, being and nothing, are used as in the lecture
"What is Metaphysics?" As a result, the question arises: how far is it possible to use the same names inside and outside of metaphysics? On this
point, Heidegger referred to the last page of *On the Way to Language:*

> We know that the possibility of an innate transformation of language
> entered Wilhelm von Humboldt's sphere of thought, from a passage in his
> treatise on 'The Diversity of the Structure of Human Language.' As his
> brother tells us in the foreword, Humboldt worked on this treatise 'lone-
> some, near a *grave'* until his death.
>
> Wilhelm von Humboldt, whose deep, dark insights into the nature of
> language we must never cease to admire, says:

>> "The *application* of an already available phonetic form to the internal
>> purposes of language . . . may be deemed possible in the middle periods
>> of *language development.* A people could, by inner illumination and favor-
>> able external circumstances, impart so different a form to the language
>> handed down to them that it would thereby turn into a wholly other,
>> wholly new language" (§10, p. 84).

> In a later passage we read:

>> "Without altering the language as regards its sounds and even less its
>> forms and laws, *time*—by a growing development of ideas, increased
>> capacity for sustained thinking, and a more penetrating sensibility—will
>> often introduce into language what it did not possess before. Then the old
>> shell is filled with a new meaning, the old coinage conveys something dif-
>> ferent, the old laws of syntax are used to hint at a differently graduated
>> sequence of ideas. All this is a lasting fruit of a people's *literature,* and
>> within literature especially of *poetry* and *philosophy*" (§11, p. 100).[89]

This text indicates what possibility there is that a metaphysical language, without changing expression, can become a non-metaphysical
language. Therefore the seminar begins with the investigation of both
conditions for this transformation:

1) "Inner illumination."
2) "Favorable external circumstances."

First, what is required for such an inner illumination to occur? Answer: that being itself announces itself, or otherwise put, that the Dasein unfolds what *Being and Time* termed an "understanding of being." The posing of the question of being *as* being in *Being and Time* amounts to such a transformation of the understanding of being that it at once calls for a renewal of language. But the language of *Being and Time*, Heidegger says, lacks assurance. For the most part, it still speaks in expressions borrowed from metaphysics and seeks to present what it wants to say with the help of new coinings, creating new words. Jean Beaufret mentions that in 1959 Hans-Georg Gadamer said of his teacher: "Hölderlin first set his tongue loose." Heidegger now says, more precisely, that through Hölderlin he came to understand how useless it is to coin new words; only after *Being and Time* was the necessity of a return to the essential simplicity of language clear to him.

Second, in respect to the "favorable conditions," two grave processes must now be examined:

a) The decline and impoverishment of language itself, which is entirely obvious if one compares the neediness of spoken language today with the riches of language still recorded by the brothers Grimm in the previous century.

b) This triggers a reverse movement that aims at setting the standard of language in the possibilities of computer calculation. The danger here lies in the fixing of language outside its natural possibilities of growth.

Roger Munier remarked that it is already a basic characteristic of the language of information science that, by a reductive analysis of all data, it sets up a new and entirely bare structure which henceforth is to function as the essence of language for all technological undertakings. In this way, language is robbed of its proper laws and immediately rendered conformable to machines. Obviously, the relation to language that makes possible such a process is determined by the conception of language as a mere instrument of information.

As far as one may surmise, the external conditions today are *unfavorable*. Between philosophy and this interpretation of language there is no longer the slightest common ground for dialogue.

What practical consequences are to be drawn from this state of affairs? In other words: what remains for the thinker to do?

The current seminar already presents a kind of response, and, Heidegger says, "that is why I am here." It is a matter for a few of us to untiringly work outside of all publicness to keep alive a thinking that is attentive to being, knowing that this work must concern itself with laying the foundation, for a distant future, of a possibility of tradition— since obviously one cannot settle a two millennia heritage in ten or twenty years.

Instead of this, "philosophy" today is satisfied with running behind science, in misrecognition of the two sole realities of this age: the development of *business* and the *armament* that this requires.

Marxism knows of these realities, but it also proposes other tasks: "The philosophers have in different ways only *interpreted* the world; it is a matter of *transforming* it."[90]

On the examination of this thesis, is there a genuine opposition between an *interpretation* and a *transformation* of the world? Is not every interpretation already a transformation of the world—assuming that this interpretation is the work of a genuine thinking? And on the other hand, does not every transformation of the world presuppose as its instrument a theoretical prediction?

Which transformation of the world do we have in Marx? That of a transformation in the conditions of production. But where does production have its place? In praxis. And praxis is determined by what? By a certain theory, which casts the concept of production as the production of the human by itself. Marx therefore has a theoretical representation of the human—a very precise representation, which includes as its foundation the Hegelian philosophy.[91]

Reversing Hegel's idealism in his own way, Marx requires that being be given precedence over consciousness. Since there is no consciousness in *Being and Time*, one could believe that there is something Heideggerian to be read here! At least Marcuse had understood *Being and Time* in this way.

For Marx, being is the production process. This is the representation that he receives from metaphysics, on the basis of Hegel's interpretation of life as process. The practical concept of production can only exist on the basis of a conception of being stemming from metaphysics.

Here again one finds the tight bond between theory and praxis, in which Auguste Comte saw two sisters. Sisters, perhaps, Heidegger says, but born from unknown parents!

Today, what does one understand by theory? Is it a programming? Program: indication, anticipatory establishment, and communication of a plan. A concert program, however, is no theory of music. In Greek, theory is θεωρία. Θεωρία names residing in the gaze of being.

In the *Nicomachean Ethics*,[92] θεωρία is the highest type of human activity; from this, it is the highest human praxis. Jean Beaufret elaborates that what is characteristic of θεωρία is to be divided into three πραγματεῖαι (activities).

Where does theory emerge more recently in a fundamental sense? With Kepler's *Cosmotheoros*, which is followed by the *Physics* of Galileo and Newton's *Principia*. And what does this concern? Galileo says this plainly: *Subjecto vetustissimo novam promovemus scientiam*. The questionable matter is movement, which Aristotle had first made into a theme as such: ἡ τοῦ δυνάμει ὄντος ἐντελέχεια ᾗ τοιοῦτον κίνησίς ἐστιν.[93]

This determination which becomes for the Scholastics *motus est actus entis in potentia pront in potentia*, is for Descartes and Pascal an occasion for ridicule. They laugh about this, however, because there no longer stands in view for them what, on the contrary, showed itself for Aristotle in all clarity: the κίνησίς, movedness *as phenomenon*. This means that the ἀλήθεια has disappeared, wherein the multiple ways of movement in their concealed unity could appear to Aristotle. Since Galileo, only a single one of these masters the entire field: the φορά. But the significance of φορά has itself changed, for the concept of place (τόπος) to which it is related, itself disappears before the positing of a body in a geometrically homogeneous space, something for which the Greeks did not even have a name. It is a matter of a mathematical project of nature on the basis of the homogeneity of space.

Why this strange project? Because nature is to become calculable, since this calculability itself is posited as the principle of a mastery of nature.

Where have we come to? The question concerning theory and practice led us here. Setting up nature as calculable and to be mastered, in the manner of Galileo, this is the new theory whose peculiarity lies in making possible the experimental method.

Indeed, what is the *ontological* significance of Galileo's and Newton's concepts of homogeneity, of the three-dimensionality of space, of change of place, etc.? This: that space and its characteristics are viewed as existing actually. This is the significance of hypothesis for Newton: I do not feign hypotheses, he says; there is nothing imaginary in them.[94]

But what occurred later with Niels Bohr and the modern physicists? They do not believe for a moment that the atomic model projected by them presents a being as such. The meaning of the word hypothesis— and thus of theory itself—has changed. It is now only an "assuming that. . . ," which is to be developed. Today it has a purely methodological meaning and no longer any ontological significance whatsoever. This by no means prevented Heisenberg from continuing to claim that he *described* nature. But what does "to describe" mean for him? In fact, the way of description is obstructed by experimentation; nature is said to be "described" from the moment that it is put into mathematical forms, the function of which is to yield exactitude while aiming at experimentation. And what is to be understood by exactitude? This is the possibility of identically repeating an experiment within the schema "if x. . . , then y." Experimentation thus concerns *the effect*. If the effect does not follow, the theory is altered. The theory is therefore essentially changeable and thus purely methodological. At bottom, it is no more than another one of the variable factors in research.

This all leads to Max Planck's thesis about being: "The real is what is measurable." The meaning of being is thus measurability, whereby it is not so much a matter of establishing "how much," but ultimately of

only serving to master and dominate the being as object. This is already
operative in the thinking of Galileo, which is even prior to the *Discours
de la Méthode.*

We are beginning to see to what extent technology is not grounded
in physics, but rather the reverse, physics is grounded upon the essence
of technology.

Supplementary elucidations regarding *effect:*

Effect means: 1) the result of that which is "previously posited" in a
theory.

2) The objective establishment of reality upon the basis of the arbitrary repeatability of an experiment.

The scientific concept of effect is explained by the proposition of the
"Second Analogy of Experience" in Kant: "Everything that happens,
that is, begins to be, presupposes something upon which it follows
according to a rule."[95] This "upon which" is to be understood expressly
in the sense of simple succession and not in the sense of a *from out of
which.* For modern physics, thunder follows lightning, and that is all.
This physics ever only observes nature as a succession of things that follow upon one another, and no longer as a course of things emerging
from each other, as was the case for Aristotle.

What for Aristotle was a development [*Auseinanderfolge*] (the result
of an emerging out of; ἐκ-εἰς), becomes a succession [*Aufeinanderfolge*]
(through the determination of the result as sequential) — this due to the
fact that the first idea is only an "occult quality," brought into disrepute
by the Cartesians, though nonetheless rehabilitated in a certain sense
by Leibniz.

September 9

Heidegger begins with a few additions to the determination of the
concept of theory, for which a start had been made in the previous session. He points out that the concept of theory developed by Newton
and Galileo stands in the middle between θεωρία in the Greek sense
and the contemporary significance of the word. From the Greek interpretation, this concept retains an ontological view of nature, which is
regarded as the totality of movement in space and time. Opposed to
this, the contemporary theory gives up this ontological tendency; it is
solely the establishing of the elements required for an experiment, or, if
one prefers, the operating instructions for carrying out an experiment.

On this, Jean Beaufret referred to *Vorträge und Aufsätze:* "The phenomena no longer appear, rather they are announced."[96] This "announcing," Heidegger explained, is to be understood in such a way that the
theory of modern physics, however operatively it might proceed, cannot
lead to a completely invented system. Instead, there must always be

reports from Nature. But these reports are no descriptions of nature. They are exclusively oriented toward the calculability of the object. As far as there is a description here, it does not consist in bringing into view the appearance of an object, but restricts itself to establishing something of nature in a mathematical formula as a law of motion.

As an example, Heidegger takes the *universal world formula*, which Heisenberg had long worked on. Insofar as this theory is possible, it could not become a description of nature; it can be only a principal analogy: what one must take into account so that, in any event, one can count on something. But what is the fundamental determination of nature for physics? Is it calculability? Then there is still the question of what is calculable. Something like energy? Again, we first need to understand this word. Actually, modern experimental physics constantly searches for the laws of motion, just as Aristotle had. This would be the meaning of the fundamental universal formula, insofar as all the possibilities of movement in their infinite variety could be deduced. Heidegger now asks what the discovery of this formula would mean for physics. The answer runs: the end of physics. Such an end would entirely alter the human situation. It would place the human being before the following decisions:

—either to open up to an entirely new relation to nature;

—or, after the work of research is concluded, to settle into the mere thoughtless exploitation of the discovery.

Here, more disturbing than the conquest of space, there appears the transformation of biology into *biophysics*. This means that the human can be produced according to a definite plan just like any other technological object. In this context, nothing is more natural than to ask whether science will be able to stop in time. Such a stop is nevertheless fundamentally impossible. To be precise, it is not a matter of ascribing limits to the human desire for knowledge, of which Aristotle spoke. The reason for this event is far rather the modern relation to *power,* a political relation. In this regard, the emergence of a new form of nationalism must be thought through, one which is grounded upon technological power and no longer (in order to give an example) on the characteristics of a people.

Here are the two hypotheses under consideration: the end of physics or the founding of a new relation to nature, assuming the discovery of a fundamental universal formula. Contemporary physicists object that the idea of this formula is very old—one had already come to believe in it at the end of the nineteenth century (Maxwell)—and that relativity theory has placed new obstacles in the way of its discovery.

Jean Beaufret responds: It is less a matter of an ontic discovery than an ontological pre-discovery. Ontologically speaking, physics is already completed.

What is decisive, Heidegger adds, is to understand that physics cannot leap beyond itself. Such a leap can just as little be accomplished by
politics, insofar as it lives today in and for the dimension of science. The
most extreme danger is that man, insofar as he produces himself, no
longer feels any other necessities than the demands of his self-production. Hence, we once again come to the question of the language of the
computer.

In these suppositions, the end of language and the end of tradition
are equally visible. What is uncanny, however, is not so much that
everything will be extinguished, but instead that this does not actually
come to light. The surge of information veils the disappearance of what
has been [*des Gewesenen*], and prospective planning is only a name for
the obstruction of the future.

As to the interest of America for the "question of being," the reality
of that country is veiled from the view of those interested: the collusion
between industry and the military (the economic development and the
armament that it requires).

But the decision does not belong to humans. If this is to become
clear, what is most important is the insight that man is not a being that
makes himself—without such an insight one remains with the supposedly political opposition between civil and industrial society, and forgets
that the concept of society is only another name, a mirror, or an extension, of subjectivity.

The Greeks had neither culture, nor religion, nor social relations.
Greek history only lasted three centuries. But essential limitation, i.e.,
finitude, is perhaps the condition of a genuine existence. For the truly
living human, there is always time.

After these thoughts on the times, Heidegger returns to a question
opened up in a previous session: how is Hegel's statement "Pure being
and pure nothing are, therefore, the same" to be distinguished from the
thesis of "What is Metaphysics?" concerning the relation between being
and nothing? Being just as much as nothing are for Hegel the Absolute
in its most extreme alienation. But for Heidegger?

The identity of being and nothing is thought in departure from the
ontological difference, but in what dimension does Hegel's determination move, when seen from the ontological difference? Hegel's proposition does not concern the ontological difference: it is an ontological
statement, as the title of Hegel's work already shows. As such, it is supported by the ontological difference. Actually the entire *Logic* is a unity
of ontological statements which are stated in a dialectical-speculative
form, whereby it is understandable that the *Logic* presents God's thought
before the creation. But what does "creation" mean? Creation is the
production of the world. In German: *Herstellung*; in Greek: ποίησις
Beings are created. Who does the production of beings require? One

must think here of the Aristotelian example of the architect. The architect creates, in that he sets out from the εἶδος. Before the creation, God thinks the εἶδος of the world, which means the totality of the categories. This is the meaning of the Hegelian ontology or "logic." As such, it presents the ontology from which God takes the measure of his creation. In Kantian terms: such is the meaning of the *intuitus originarius.*

Viewed from the ontological difference, Hegel's statement moves along one side of the difference: the ontological side. It has to utter the being of beings, which since Kant is the objectivity of the object.

What occurs with the nothing in "What is Metaphysics?" From what place can Heidegger say:

Being : Nothing : The Same?

From a question concerning the essence of metaphysics, that itself is nothing metaphysical. Heidegger's word belongs neither on the side of beings, nor simply on that of being, it speaks from where the horizon of the difference itself becomes visible. If one will allow, the ontological difference is the condition of possibility for metaphysics, the place upon which it is grounded.

But what is the theme of the Heideggerian proposition? It is difference itself. Heidegger speaks of the difference, without holding onto it; thereby he has abandoned metaphysics. One can now ask, what is characteristic of the nothing just spoken of? If it is nothing negative, then by what is it distinguished? Heidegger says: it is a nihilating nothing [*nichtendes Nichts*]. The essence of the nothing consists in the turning away from beings, in the distance from them. Only in this distance can the being as such become apparent. The nothing is not the simple negation of the being. On the contrary, the nothing in its nihilation refers to the being in its manifestation. The nihilation of the nothing "is" being.

The intention of the lecture, held before a gathering of scientists and faculty, was thus: to show the scientists that there is something other than the object of their exclusive occupations and that this other precisely first enables that very thing with which they are preoccupied.

With this, the concluding sentence of the lecture, which poses the basic question of metaphysics, is clarified: "Why are there beings at all and not, far rather, nothing?"

This sentence is none other than the question posed by Leibniz. But the Leibnizian answer is theological. It limits itself to referring to the supreme being, the creator of the best of all possible worlds.

Heidegger's question, on the contrary, does not inquire after the first cause, but rather seeks to come out of the forgetfulness of being. It authentically says: how does it come about that you concern yourselves so much with beings and so little with being?

In human thinking, why do beings press into the foreground? Whence the forgetfulness, the nihilating nothing? In other words: what decrees the dominance of the "fall upon beings"? "Fall" is not to be understood ontically as a *falling away from* (or as a plunge), but rather, ontologically as an essential determination of everyday Dasein. This ontologically understood "fall" is just the natural condition of Dasein, insofar as it is only able to concern itself with things, by not letting itself into being. But the concern with beings is possible and understandable only through a departure from being. If being necessarily remains unthematized in human life, if, in other words, the aim of *Being and Time* does not lead everyday Dasein to a thematization of being—something which would not constitute its ownness anyway—it nevertheless remains the case that "human life" as such would not be possible without the prior and unacknowledged clearing of being.

This is the meaning of the celebrated and yet misunderstood analysis of equipmentality in *Being and Time*. The equipmental character of the thing does not need to become thematized in order to exist, and nevertheless, it is in the chair *as* chair that I am seated.

September 11

On the distinction between negating [*Nichten*] and denying [*Verneinen*]: is this covered by the Greek distinction between οὐκ and μή? If negating belongs to the Greek οὐκ, then *nothing* signifies total nothingness (*nihil negativum*); beings are simply denied: there are no beings. If, on the contrary, one understands the nothing in negating according to the meaning of μή, then it should indicate a certain defect in regard to being. But if being and nothing are the same, then the nothing in question cannot signify a lack. Therefore, one should not understand negating in a privative-negative way. It is a matter of something other, completely specific and unique.

We keep the guiding statement ever in view:

Being : Nothing : The Same

Nothing is a characteristic of being. It is not a being, but this in a manner that is thoroughly different from the sentence: The being is not (which would be an ontic proposition). On the contrary, one says: the nothing characterizes being, this is therefore an ontological proposition. Viewed from the ontic horizon, being is precisely not some being; viewed from the categories, it *is* not. Otherwise said: insofar as the nothing and its negating are not understood negatively, being is something entirely other than a being. It is essential to the participle form "nihilating" [*nichtend*] that the participle show a determinate "activity" of being, through which alone the particular being *is*. One can name it an origin, assuming that all ontic-causal overtones are excluded: it is the event [*Ereignis*] of being as condition for the arrival of beings: being lets beings presence.

It is a matter here of understanding that the deepest meaning of being is *letting*. Letting the being be, this is the non-causal meaning of "letting" in "Time and Being." This "letting" is something fundamentally different from "doing." The text "Time and Being" attempted to think this "letting" still more originarily as "giving."

The *giving* meant here speaks in the expression *Es gibt* ["There is"] (usually translated by *"Il y a,"* regarding which Heidegger explained that *"Il y a"* is too ontic insofar as it refers to the presence of beings).

"Es gibt":

Es gibt, in Latin: *habet.* Constructed with the accusative it expresses an ontic relation.

Here one must take pains to avoid possible errors. For as we have just seen, the expression *"Es gibt"* is not safe from an ontic conception. We note therefore:

1) It is tempting to understand *"Es gibt"* as meaning "It lets [something] come to presence." And through this emphasis upon letting come to presence, the giving in *"Es gibt"* is ontically conceived. Hence, if I say in French: there are trout in this stream [*Il y a des truites dans ce ruisseau*], the *"Il y a"* is understood in regard to the presence of beings, to their presenting [*Anwesung*] — and the "to let come to presence" is already on the verge of being understood as "to make present." Heard in this way, the *"Es gibt"* is grasped ontically so that the emphasis lies upon the fact of being.

2) But if the *"Es gibt"* is thought in regard to an interpretation of the letting itself, then the emphasis changes.

Presence is no longer emphasized, but rather the *letting* itself. *"Es gibt"* then has the precise meaning: *"to let* the presencing." Thus it is no longer the presence of a being which draws one's attention, but the ground which that being covers over, in order to make itself independent from it: letting as such, the gift of a "giving which gives only its gift, but in the giving holds itself back and withdraws."[97]

Now a possibility is perhaps offered to find a way out of the insoluble difficulty which here tempts one to say "the impossible": "Being is." Perhaps one should sooner say, "There is being" [*"Es gibt Sein"*], in the sense of, "it *lets* being" [*"Es läßt Sein"*].

We can say, in summary,[98] that three meanings can be emphasized in "letting-be."

The first refers to that which is (to the being). Over against this first sense, there stands another sense for which the attention is drawn less towards *what* is given (towards what is), than towards *the presencing* itself. It then concerns an interpretation of being of the sort given by metaphysics.

Within this second emphasis, however, a third has its place, where the stress is now decisively placed upon the *letting* itself, that which *allows* the presencing. Since it allows (releases?) presencing, which means that it allows being, this third emphasis points to the ἐποχή of being. In this third meaning, one stands before being *as* being, and no longer before one of the forms of its destiny.

If the emphasis is: *to let* presencing, there is no longer room for the very name of being. *Letting* is then the pure *giving*, which itself refers to the it [*das Es*] that gives, which is understood as *Ereignis*.

After the seminar reached this point, it attempted to make the word *Ereignis* understandable.

The first remark makes clear that the French word *avènement* [advent] is entirely inadequate for translating *Ereignis*. The French translation proposed for "Time and Being" is again adopted; *Ereignis:* the *appropriement* [enowning].

It is then asked: what relation does enowning have to ontological difference? How is enowning to be said? How does it fit into the history of being? Is being supposed to be the countenance of enowning for the Greeks? Finally, is it possible to say: "Being is enowned through enowning" ["*Sein ist durch das Ereignis ereignet*"]? Answer: yes.

In order to take a few small steps into these difficult questions (which remain all too difficult as long as their understanding is not sufficiently prepared), let us first consider a few indications that could help us discern various and yet convergent paths of access to the *question* of enowning.

–The most appropriate text for a clarification of this question is the lecture "The Principle of Identity," which is even better heard than read.[99]

–An excellent way of approaching enowning would be to look into the essence of positionality [*Ge-stell*], insofar as it is a passage from metaphysics to another thinking ("a Janus head" it is called in *On Time and Being*[100]), for positionality is essentially ambiguous. "The Principle of Identity" already says: positionality (the gathering unity of all ways of positing [*Weisen des stellens*]) is the completion and consummation of metaphysics and at the same time the disclosive preparation of enowning. This is why it is by no means a question of viewing the advent of technology as negative occurrence (but just as little as a positive occurrence in the sense of a paradise on Earth).

–Positionality is, as it were, the photographic negative of enowning.

–Thinking enowning with the concepts of being and the history of being will not be successful; nor will it be with the assistance of the Greek (which is precisely something "to go beyond"). With being, the ontological difference also vanishes. Looking ahead, one would likewise have to view the continual references to the ontological difference from 1927 to 1936 as a necessary impasse [*Holzweg*].

–With enowning, it is no longer an issue of Greek thought at all, and what is most astonishing here is that Greek continues to retain its essential signification, while it is *at the same time* no longer able to speak as a language. Perhaps the difficulty lies in that language speaks too quickly. Hence the attempt to remain *On the Way to Language.*

–In enowning, the history of being has not so much reached its end, as that it now appears *as* history of being. There is no destinal epoch of enowning. Sending is from enowning [*Das Schicken ist aus dem Ereignen*].

–Certainly one can say: enowning enowns being [*das Ereignis ereignet das Sein*] but it is to be noted that for the Greeks, being *as* being was neither thought nor raised as a question. The return to the Greeks only has meaning as a return to being.

–The "step back" (the step that retreats from metaphysics) has the sole meaning of enabling, in the gathering of thinking upon itself, a glance ahead to what comes. It means that thinking begins anew, so that in the essence of technology it catches sight of the heralding portent, the covering pre-appearance, the concealing pre-appearing of enowning itself.

We will now attempt to bring into the open this pre-appearing of enowning under the veil of positionality.

The beginning must be made by a return to the history of being. The various epochs of the history of being–the various and successive self-withdrawals of being in its destiny–are the epochs of the various ways in which presence destines itself to western man. If one considers one of these sendings, as it was destined to man in the nineteenth and twentieth centuries, what does it consist of?

The manner of this sending is *objectivity* [*Gegenständlichkeit*] (as the objective being of the object). Now the further that modern technology unfolds, the more does objectivity transform into *standing reservedness* (into a holding-at-one's-disposal). Already today there are no longer objects (no beings, insofar as these would stand against a subject taking them into view)–there are now only standing reserves (beings that are held in readiness for being consumed). In French one could perhaps say: there are no longer any *substances* [substances], but rather only *subsistances* [means of subsistence] in the sense of "supplies." Hence the energy politics and the politics of agriculture, which indeed no longer have anything to do with objects, but rather with the systematic ordering of a space within a general planning, directed towards future exploitation. Everything (beings as a whole) from the outset arranges itself in the horizon of utility, the dominance, or better yet, the *orderability* of what is to be seized. The forest ceases to be an object (as it was

for the scientists of the eighteenth and nineteenth centuries), and becomes, for the human—finally stepping forth in his true form as *tech-
nologist,* i.e., for the human who a priori sees the particular being in the
horizon of usability–a "greenspace." It can no longer appear in the
objective neutrality of an over against [*Gegenüber*]. There is no longer
anything other than standing reserves: stock, supplies, means.

The ontological determination of standing reserve (of the being as
material supply) is not permanence (the steady persistence), but rather
orderability, the constant possibility of being summoned and ordered,
that is, the persistent standing-at-one's-disposal. In orderability, the
particular being is *posited* from the ground up and exclusively as *disposable*—disposable for consumption in the planning of the whole.

One of the essential moments in the way of being of contemporary
beings (in disposability according to a plan-driven consumption) is replaceability, the fact that—in a game that has become universal and
where anything can take the place of anything else—every being becomes essentially *replaceable.* The industry of "consumer" products and
the predominance of the replacement make this empirically obvious.

Today being is being-replaceable. Already the idea of "repair" has
become an "anti-economical" thought. It is essential for every being of
consumption that it *be already* consumed and thus call for its replacement. We have here one of the forms of the atrophy of the traditional, of
what is transmitted from generation to generation. Even in the phenomenon of fashion, what is essential is no longer *embellishment* and
adornment (fashion as embellishment has thus become just as anachro-
nistic as mending), but instead the replaceability of models from season
to season. A piece of clothing is no longer changed as soon as and because it has become damaged, but rather because it has the essential
character of being "the outfit of the moment in expectation of the next."

In regards to *time,* this characteristic results in *current affairs.* Persistence [*Dauer*] is no longer the constancy of the traditional, but rather
the continual novelty of incessant change. Did the slogans of May 1968
against consumer society go so far as to recognize in consumption the
current countenance of being?

Only modern technology makes possible the production of all these
economic standing-reserves. It is more than a fundamental condition,
it is the ground itself and therefore its horizon; hence that artificial material which increasingly replaces the "natural" material. There, too,
nature withdraws as nature . . .

It is not sufficient, however, to determine these realities ontically.
What stands in question is that *modern man finds himself henceforth in a
fundamentally new relation to being*—AND THAT HE KNOWS NOTHING
OF IT.

In positionality, the human is challenged forth to comport himself in correspondence with exploitation and consumption; the relation to exploitation and consumption requires the human to *be* in this relationship. Man does not hold technology in his hand. He is its plaything. In this situation, there reigns a complete forgetfulness of being, a complete concealment of being. Cybernetics becomes a replacement for philosophy and poetry. Political science, sociology, and psychology become prioritized, disciplines which no longer bear the slightest relation to their own foundation. In this regard, modern man is a slave to the forgetfulness of being.

Through this, the state of affairs becomes visible (as far as it will let itself be seen) that the human is "used by being" [*utilisé*]. In the word "to use" [*Brauchen*] we hear an echo of the χρή of Parmenides and Anaximander. It thoroughly corresponds to "*utilisé*," but in the sense that one has need of that which one "uses."

Thus the human necessarily belongs to, and has his place in, the openness (and currently in the forgetfulness) of being. Being, however, for its opening, needs man as the there of its manifestation.

For this reason the letter to Jean Beaufret[101] speaks of man as the *shepherd* of being—let us note that here for once the French speaks more clearly than the German: *berger* [shepherd] is the one who *beherbergt* [*héberge*] (provides shelter [*Obhut*]).[102] The human is the placeholder of the nothing.

If being needs something of the human's kind in order to be, then a *finitude of being* must accordingly be assumed; that consequently being would not be absolutely for itself, this is the most pointed contradiction to Hegel. For indeed when Hegel says that the Absolute is not "without us," he says this only in regard to the Christian "God who needs humans." For Heidegger's thinking, on the contrary, being is not without its relation to Dasein.[103]

Nothing is further away from Hegel and all idealism.

Seminar in Zähringen 1973

I

September 6

After the Thor seminars, the Freiburg seminar begins. Whereas in 1968 and 1969 an access to the question of Being was attempted on the basis of Hegel and Kant, here such an access is attempted on the basis of Husserl.

The point of departure is a letter from Jean Beaufret, in which two questions are raised:

1) To what extent can it be said that there is no question of Being in Husserl?

2) In what sense is Heidegger able to call his analysis of environment[104] an "essential gain"[105] and yet claim elsewhere that it "remains of subordinate significance."[106]

The work begins by the examination of the second question.

The analysis of the worldhood of the world is indeed an "essential step" to the extent that, for the first time in the history of philosophy, being-in-the-world appears as the primary mode of encountering entities. Better: being-in-the-world is discovered as the primary and irreducible *fact*, always already given, and thus radically "prior" to any conception of consciousness.

Yet this analysis "remains of subordinate significance." To understand in what sense this is the case, one need only recall the "guiding aim" of *Being and Time:* "to raise anew *the question of the meaning of being.*"[107] To be clear, one must then say: the analysis of the worldhood of the world within Heidegger's project is only the "concrete" way of approaching the project itself. As such, the project includes this analysis as nothing more than a means, which remains subordinate in relation to the project. In other words, to read paragraphs 14 to 24 of *Being and Time* for themselves (detached from the plan of the whole) could well be a fundamental misunderstanding with respect to the attempt made by Heidegger.

One always needs, therefore, to return to the core of this thought, i.e., the question of being. The first question posed by Jean Beaufret leads back to it directly: to what extent can it be said that there is no question of being in Husserl? What does "question of being" mean? It means the question concerning the meaning of being. Heidegger explains still more precisely: after *Being and Time*, the expression "meaning" is replaced by "truth" — so that the question of Being, now understood as the question concerning the truth of Being, can no longer be taken as a metaphysical question.

Indeed, metaphysics investigates the being of beings. What is proper to Heidegger's question is a view to the being of being [*Sein des Seins*], if one can express it in this way. Better: the *truth* of being, where truth is to be understood from preserving, in which being is safeguarded as being. In this rigorous sense, there is no question of being in Husserl. Indeed, Husserl considers problems that are more strictly metaphysical, for instance, the problem of categories.

However, Heidegger indicates, Husserl touches upon or struggles with the question of being in chapter six of the sixth *Logical Investigation*, with the notion of "categorial intuition." The first step of our work is thus clearly delineated: to understand in what sense the notion of "categorial intuition" is for Heidegger the focal point of Husserlian thought.

The initial question is how did Husserl arrive at "categorial intuition"? To reconstruct this path, the place of categorial intuition must be precisely situated. The second section of the sixth *Logical Investigation* is entitled "Sense and Understanding." Chapter six, which opens this second section, bears the title "Sensuous and Categorial Intuition." One can therefore say that in order to arrive at categorial intuition, Husserl begins with sensuous intuition.

But what is sensuous intuition? What is Husserl's point of departure when he analyzes sensuous intuition? Jean Beaufret recalls at this point the celebrated Husserlian example: the "inkwell." Heidegger: "Is it an inkwell?" No, it is not; in the context of Husserl's reflection, the inkwell can only be apprehended as something else. To be precise: the inkwell only operates here as an object of sensuous perception.

But what is the ground of the sensuous perception? On what is the sensuous object grounded, insofar as it is sensuous?

The ground of the sensuous is what Husserl calls the *hyle*, which means, that which affects sensibly, in short, the sense data (blue, black, spatial extension, etc.). What is perceived sensibly? The sense data themselves. Now *along with* these sense data, an *object* becomes visible in perception. The object is not given in the sensuous impression. The objectivity of the object cannot be perceived sensibly. In summary, the fact that the object is an object does not arise from a sensuous intuition.

And yet this object is in fact perceived. In the language of the philosophical tradition, this object is called a thing. A thing is a *substance*. For Kant, substance is one of the categories of the understanding. This means, if we recall the "Copernican revolution," that the *thing* is adjusted in advance to the power of knowing, or that, in advance, the category "substance" brings the manifold of hyletic data into a definite form. Thus, through knowledge, which for Kant is the activity of bringing-into-form that is accomplished by the understanding, the object is posited as a synthesis of intuition and concept.

In contrast with Kant, for whom the bringing-into-form is only, as

concept, a function of the understanding, Husserl will attempt to articulate what Kant simply characterizes as the concept of form. Now the
Kantian idea of intuition directly leads to the idea of a *given* to intuition.
The expression of *categorial intuition* clearly indicates that the category
would be more than a form. Indeed, categorial intuition strictly says: an
intuition that brings a category to view. Or else: an intuition (a being-
present for) which is immediately *directed to* a category.

With the expression of categorial intuition, Husserl succeeds in
thinking the categorial as *given*.

I see this book before me. But where is the substance in this book? I
do not see it in the same way that I see the book. And yet this book is a
substance that I must "see" in some fashion, otherwise I could not see
anything at all. We encounter here the Husserlian idea of "surplus"
[*Überschuss*].[108] Heidegger explains: the "is," through which I observe
the presence of the inkwell as object or substance, is a "surplus" in relation to the sensuous affections. But in a certain respect the "is" is given
in the same manner as the sensuous affections: the "is" is not added to the
sense data; it is "seen" — even if it is *seen* differently from what is sensibly visible. In order to be "seen" in this way, it *must* be *given*.

For Husserl, the categorial (that is, the Kantian forms) is just as
given as the sensuous. There is therefore a thoroughly CATEGORIAL
INTUITION.

Here the initial question returns: by what path did Husserl arrive at
categorial intuition? The answer is unmistakable: since categorial intuition is *similar* to sensuous intuition (namely, as giving), Husserl reaches
categorial intuition by way of an *analogy*. In an analogy, something gives
the measure for the correspondence. In the analogy between the two types
of intuition, what corresponds to what? Answer: the sense data are what
gives the measure, and the categorial is what corresponds to the sense
data. Categorial intuition is "made analogous" to sensuous intuition.

What is telling in this analogy is that the categorial, the forms, the
"is," are able to be encountered, that they are given accessibly —
whereas with Kant they are only deduced from the table of judgments.
For Kant, everything follows the guiding thread of the judgment
(which comes to him from the logical tradition), without ever encountering the *fact of the category* — that is, the fact that the category can be
encountered just like something given to the senses.

At this point, Heidegger cites the sentence: "I *see* white paper and *say*
'white paper,' thereby expressing, with precise adequacy, only what I
see."[109]

What is Husserl's decisive discovery, and at the same time his fundamental difficulty?

I see white paper. But this is a twofold seeing; there are two visions:
sensuous vision and categorial vision. The difficulty lies in the double

signification of *seeing*—a double signification that already governs Plato's philosophy. The difficulty consists in that if I see white paper, I do not see the substance in the same way "as" I see the white paper. Antisthenes already expressed this difficulty for Plato: ὦ Πλάτον, ἵππον μὲν ὁρῶ, ἱππότητα δὲ οὐκ ὁρῶ. ("O Plato, I surely see the horse, but I do not see horsehood.")[110]

Once more: when I see this book, I do see a substantial thing, without however seeing the substantiality as I see the book. But it is the substantiality that, in its non-appearence, enables what appears to appear. In this sense, one can even say that it is more apparent than what itself appears.

This is Husserl's decisive contribution, which was an essential impetus for Heidegger. But precisely in what way?

We must constantly emphasize that the only question which has ever moved Heidegger is the question of being: what does "being" mean? Now in the entire philosophical tradition (except in its earliest Greek beginning), the sole fundamental determination of being is that of the copula of a judgment—one which, as Heidegger remarks, is a correct, but nonetheless untrue determination. With his analyses of the categorial intuition, Husserl freed being from its attachment to judgment.[111] By doing so, the entire field of investigation is re-oriented. If I pose the question of the meaning of being, Heidegger says, I must already be beyond being, understood as the being of beings. More precisely still: in the question concerning the meaning of being, what I ask about [*das Befragte*] is being, that is to say, the being of beings; that towards which I am inquiring [*das Erfragte*] is the meaning of being—which later will be called the truth of being.

In order to unfold the question concerning the meaning of being, being must be *given* in order to inquire after its meaning. Husserl's achievement consists in just this making present of being, which is phenomenally present in the category. Through this achievement, Heidegger adds, I finally had the ground: "being" is no mere concept, no pure abstraction arising by way of deduction. The point that Husserl does not cross, however, is this: after having reached, as it were, being as *given*, he does not inquire any further into it. He does not unfold the question: "what does being mean?" For Husserl, there was not the slightest possibility of a question, since for him it goes without saying that "being" means being-object.

Here it is not Husserl, but Heidegger who brings a decisive characterization: objectivity is a mode of presence. Precisely stated, objectivity is being-present in the dimension or "space" of subjectivity, whether it is a matter of (with Kant) the subjectivity of a finite subject, or (with Hegel) the subjectivity of the absolute subject, who, in the knowledge of itself, penetrates the object just as much as the subject, as well as the relation between the two.

But from what standpoint can Heidegger make this characterization? From a questioning and thorough thinking of Plato and Aristotle. Indeed, in Plato and Aristotle's texts, for those who know that being is not an abstract concept, there is the first determination of the being of beings, a fundamental determination for the entirety of philosophical thinking: being, that is, presencing. Neither Plato nor Aristotle put into question this determination, which for them is simply *manifest*.

The entire history of metaphysics is organized from here as the succession of the various fundamental figures of the being of beings, on the basis of the original determination where "being" is apprehended as παρουσία.

Thus the entire history of metaphysics proves itself to be the history of the being of beings.

Accordingly, one is at first glance in an apparently ambiguous relationship with the history of metaphysics:

— On the one hand, metaphysics never asks about anything other than being;

— On the other hand, it never asks about the *meaning* of being.

From this ambiguity arises the temptation to take philosophy as posing, at each of its epochs, the fundamental question concerning the *meaning* of being. In the perspective of the work to come, Heidegger invites the participants of the seminar to reflect on the question: Can one say that the question concerning the meaning of being was ever posed in the entire history of philosophy? We cannot be satisfied in simply answering that it has never occurred.

The session ends with a return to the Husserlian idea of the "sensibly given"—this time in the perspective of what these givens become in *Being and Time*.

Being and Time no longer speaks of consciousness. Consciousness is plain and simply set aside—for Husserl this was a pure scandal! Instead of "consciousness" we find Dasein. But what does Dasein mean? And which is grounded in the other?

We need to inquire here into the meaning of consciousness [*Bewußtsein*]. In consciousness, there is knowing [*Wissen*], which is related to *videre*, in the sense that knowing is having-seen. Consciousness moves in the domain of sight, where it is illuminated by the *lumen naturale*. What does the light "do"? It brings clarity. And what does clarity make possible? First and foremost, that I can encounter things. The French verb *regarder* (to look at) is here very telling. *Regarder* indeed means *garder*, to preserve, to safe-guard [*ge-wahren; re-garder*], in the sense of letting what I am looking at come near me.

What is the basis of this having-seen for any consciousness? The fundamental possibility for the human being to traverse an open expanse in order to reach the things.

This being-in-an-open-expanse is what *Being and Time* called (Heidegger even adds: "very awkwardly and in an unhelpful way") Dasein.

Dasein must be understood as being-the-clearing. The *Da* is namely the word for the open expanse.

We can see clearly here that consciousness is rooted in Dasein, and not the other way around.

Consciousness and Dasein [*Bewußtsein und Dasein*]: both words contain the verb "being" [*Sein*]. Today's seminar closes with the question: what is the meaning of being in consciousness and Dasein? This is the task for tomorrow.

II

Today's session, Friday September 7, 1973, begins with the reading of the protocol.

Thereafter, Heidegger notes that many additions could be made to what was discussed the first day. But his concern in this seminar is something quite other. This is why he will restrict himself to two observations, with the goal of avoiding any over-simplification.

With respect to Kant, mention was made yesterday of an abstract deduction of categories. Heidegger questions: is there not in the Kantian doctrine something more and other than abstraction and deducability, in regard to the ways in which these are understandable and perceivable? Jean Beaufret mentions here the "schematism." In the schematism, Kant brings the categories and time into a relation, which is—Heidegger says in passing—the Kantian way of discussing being and time.

With respect now to Husserl, Heidegger asks in what context the *Logical Investigations* come to categorial intuition. It is important to note that it is not in the context of an elaboration of the problem of categories—that is, the metaphysical problem of being. On the contrary, the relation of analogy between understanding and sensibility forms this context, each understood in that unity where the constitution of the object as object of experience becomes possible. It is thus a problematic of the theory of experience—through which Husserl again continues the Kantian heritage.

Within this context, Heidegger emphasizes, categorial intuition appears without in any way arising from an explicit ontological thematic.

These two remarks, as we can see, rectify yesterday's discussion, or better, they prevent us from understanding it in a unilateral fashion. The fact that in Kant the categories are deduced in no way implies that the categorial is abstracted in isolation from any possible "concreteness." The fact that the categorial is immediately and concretely encountered in Husserl, in no way means that Husserl can unfold the question of the truth of being.

This clarification made, the projected course of the seminar can resume, with a return to the question posed at the end of the last session: What is the relation between consciousness [*Bewußt-sein*] and Dasein (better yet: between the being-of-consciousness and being-the-there-of-the-open-expanse)?

For an appropriate discussion of the question, the meaning of the verb "to be" in both words must be clarified. In French, the word *conscience* is not composed with the verb "to be." Nonetheless *conscience* includes a character of being. Which one? When I say: "I am conscious," there is said along with this: I am conscious of myself. The being-conscious-of-oneself, this being-character of consciousness, is determined by subjectivity. But subjectivity itself is not questioned in regards to its being; since Descartes, it is the *fundamentum inconcussum*. In the entirety of modern thought, stemming from Descartes, subjectivity thus constitutes the barrier to the unfolding of the question of being.

If we inquire into the character of the presence [*Gegenwärtigkeit*] that reigns in the "making-present-to-oneself," which every consciousness is, we must admit that this making-present-to-oneself takes place in *immanence*. Whatever I am conscious of, it is present to me—which means: it is *in* subjectivity, *in* my consciousness.

If one adds intentionality to consciousness, then the intended object still has its place in the immanence of consciousness.

In *Being and Time*, on the contrary, the "thing" has its place no longer in consciousness, but *in the world* (which again is itself not immanent to consciousness).

Thus, despite intentionality, Husserl remains trapped in immanence —and the consequence of this position are the *Méditations cartésiennes*.

Certainly, Husserl's fundamental position is a step ahead of neo-Kantianism, in which the object is no longer a sensuous multiplicity organized by the concepts of the understanding. With Husserl, the object retrieves its proper consistency; Husserl saves the object, but by situating it in the immanence of consciousness.

With Husserl, the sphere of consciousness is not challenged, much less shattered. Heidegger adds: one cannot, in fact, shatter it as long as one starts from the *ego cogito*; for it is the basic constitution of the *ego cogito* (just as with the monad in Leibniz) to have no windows from which something could either enter or exit. In this way, the *ego cogito* is an enclosed space. The idea of "exiting" this enclosed space is itself contradictory. This is why one needs to start from something other than the *ego cogito*.

Heidegger's point of departure is simply other. One could even call it, at first glance, less refined: When I look at the inkwell, he says, I take it itself into view, the inkwell itself, without reference to some hyletic data and categories. It is an issue of undergoing a fundamental experience with the thing itself. It is impossible to undergo such an experience by starting from consciousness. For such an experience, one needs a domain other than consciousness. It is this other domain that was called Da-sein.

Now, what does the word "being" mean when one speaks of Dasein? In contrast with the immanence to consciousness expressed by "being" in consciousness [*Bewusst*-sein], "being" in Da-*sein* says being-outside-of. . . . The domain in which everything that can be termed a thing is encounterable as such is a region which grants the possibility for that thing to manifest itself "outside." The being in Da-sein must preserve an "outside." This is why the mode of being of Dasein is characterized in *Being and Time* by ek-stasis. Da-sein thus rigorously means: ek-statically being the there.

Immanence, here, is broken through and through.

Dasein is essentially ek-static. One must understand this ek-static character not only with respect to that which presences, in the sense of what holds its place over against us, but also as ek-stasis in relation to the past, to the present, and to the future.

In the expression Da-sein, "being" thus means the ek-stasis of ek-sistence.

Here it is important to recognize the impetus that Heidegger received from the Husserlian notion of intentionality. After receiving this impetus, Heidegger's work consisted in the investigation of what is originally contained in intentionality. Now, to think intentionality through to its ground means: to ground it in the ek-stasis of Da-sein. In a word, one needs to recognize that consciousness is grounded in Da-sein.

Today, Heidegger adds, I would formulate this relation differently. I would no longer speak simply of ek-stasis, but of instancy in the clearing [*Inständigkeit in der Lichtung*]. This expression must in turn be understood as the unity of two senses:

— standing in the three ek-stases.

— guarding and maintaining being through the entirety of Dasein.

Thus, the radically different senses of *being* in consciousness and Dasein are clarified. From this, one can measure to what extent, in a thought centered on Da-sein, the status of all that it encounters is transformed. From now on, man is ek-statically face to face with what is as such—and no longer with the mediation of a representation (which, by definition, presents a shadow of what is). Heidegger explains by posing the question: when, in my memory, I think of René Char at the Busclats, who or what is thereby given to me?

René Char himself! And not God knows what "image" through which I would be mediately related to him.

This is so simple that it is extremely difficult to explain philosophically. Basically, Heidegger adds, it is not yet understood at all. A participant in the seminar intervenes: is not the passage from consciousness to Dasein originally the "revolution of the mode of thinking" of which Kant spoke, or the "reversal of all modes and forms of representation" of which Hölderlin spoke?[112] Heidegger rectifies: It would be better to speak of a revolution of the location of thinking. Further, instead of "revolution," this should be understood simply as *displacement* [Ortsverlegung], in that original sense in which the thought engaged in *Being and Time* displaces what philosophy has placed *in* consciousness. It is then noted that it is philosophy that, situating the place in consciousness, *dis*-places [ver*legt*] everything, by replacing what Heidegger calls Da-sein by that self-enclosed place which is consciousness. Here finally the relation between consciousness and Da-sein is presented in its full scope. Here one can understand what it means to say that consciousness is grounded in Da-sein.

At this point, recalling the text "My Way Into Phenomenology,"[113] Heidegger returns to Husserl. He underlines that Husserl's philosophical point of departure was Franz Brentano, the author of *Psychology from an Empirical Standpoint*. Now, my own point of departure, he remarks, was the same Franz Brentano—but not this work of 1874; it was far rather in *On the Manifold Meaning of Being in Aristotle* (1862, Freiburg) that Heidegger learned to read philosophy. A strange and significant commonality between Husserl and Heidegger, who both took their first steps with the same philosopher, but not with the same book. My Brentano, Heidegger says with a smile, is the Brentano of Aristotle!

Why stress this difference? To clarify the difference between Greek thought and the scholastic-modern thought. All the attempts to precisely situate this difference must take the utmost care and employ rigorous terminology. Thus, Heidegger reports, Romano Guardini sought to name the particularity of Greek thought and spoke of a thought "more objective" than modern thought. Now, this term "objectivity" can in no way characterize Greek thought. First, there is no word in Greek that says "what stands against" [*Gegenstand*] — "*object*." For Greek thought, there is no object, but instead that which, from itself, presences.

On the question as to whether, despite everything, one could understand object in the above named sense, Heidegger answers that it is impossible, since the object is constituted by representation. The representation, namely, that is prior in regards to the object, posits the object across from it, in such a way that the object is never able to first presence from itself.

One must therefore leave the domain of consciousness and its representations if one wants to think what the Greeks thought.

To leave the region of consciousness and attain that of Da-sein: and thus to see that, understood as Da-sein (that is, from the ek-static), the human only exists in coming from itself to what is wholly other than itself, in coming to the clearing of being.

This clearing—Heidegger points to the difficulty here of saying this—this free dimension, is not the creation of man, it is not man. On the contrary, it is that which is assigned to him, since it is addressed to him: it is that which is destined to him.

On this point, Heidegger refers to the essay on "The Origin of the Work of Art" and to the discussions of the Fourfold, for instance in the lecture "The Thing," in *Vorträge und Aufsätze.*[114] It is essential to see that, in its new location, thinking abandons from the outset the primacy of consciousness, along with its consequence, the primacy of man. It was already said in "The Letter on Humanism," in reference to a statement from Sartre (*"Précisément nous sommes sur un plan où il y a seulement des hommes"*[115]): "Instead of this, thought from *Being and Time*, we should say: *précisément nous sommes sur un plan où il y a principalement l'Être.*"[116]

This is to be shown in the next step of the work, and, indeed, from a position of extreme opposition. Heidegger opens the volume of Marx's *Early Writings* and reads the following sentence, taken from the "Contribution to the critique of Hegel's Philosophy of Right": "To be radical is to grasp the root of the matter. But for man the root is man himself."[117]

Marxism as a whole rests upon this thesis, Heidegger explains. Indeed, Marxism thinks on the basis of production: social production of society (society produces itself) and the self-production of the human being as a social being. Thinking in this manner, Marxism is indeed the thought of today, where the self-production of man and society plainly prevails.

I would like to maintain, or rather presume, Heidegger says, that the self-production of man raises the danger of self-destruction.

What are we witnessing, in truth? What is it that reigns today, determining the reality of earth as a whole?

The imperative of progress. This imperative of progress demands an imperative of production that is combined with an imperative of ever-new needs. The imperative of ever-new needs is of such a sort that everything which is imperatively new is likewise immediately obsolete and outmoded, replaced by something "even newer," and so forth. In this rush, every possibility of tradition is broken. What has been can no longer be present—except in the form of the *outmoded*, which as a result is entirely inconsequential.

If it is granted that it is man who brings about all of this, the question arises: Could man ever break the domination of these imperatives himself?

Marxism and sociology name the constraints of today's reality "imperatives."

Heidegger gathers them under the name of positionality [*Ge-stell*]. Positionality is the gathering, the totality of all the modes of positing which are imposed upon the human being to the extent that it ek-sists today. Thus positionality is in no way the product of human machination. It is, on the contrary, the most extreme form of the history of metaphysics, that is, of the destiny of being. Within this destiny, man has gone from the epoch of objectivity to that of orderability: in such an epoch, which is now ours, everything and every means of calculation are constantly at the disposal of an ordering. Strictly speaking, there are no longer objects; only "consumer goods" at the disposal of every consumer, who is himself situated in the market of production and consumption.

According to Marx, the man who is for himself his own root is indeed the man of this production and of the consumption that belongs to it. This is the man of our present.

But man understood as Da-sein, ek-static instancy in the clearing of being, stands the proposition of the Marxian statement on its head. Can one then say that for Heidegger it is Da-sein that would be the root of man? No. The concept of "root" makes it impossible to express the relation of man to being.

We return to the question mentioned earlier: the man of the times, the man who understands himself and acts as the producer of all "reality," the man who finds himself today caught in the increasingly constraining network of the socio-economic "imperatives" (which are, seen from the history of being, the precipitates of positionality), can that man himself produce the means of working a way out of the pressure of the "imperatives"?

How could he manage this without surrendering his own determination as *producer* ? And is such a surrender possible in the horizon of today's reality? What would such a renunciation signify? It would mean renouncing progress itself, committing to a general restriction of consumption and production. A simple and immediately intuitive example: in the perspective of this renunciation, "tourism" would no longer be possible, instead one would restrict oneself and remain at home.

Now is there still, in these times, something like an "at home," a dwelling, an abode? No, there are "dwelling machines," urban population centers, in short: the industrialized product, but no longer a *home*.

All these questions we are considering, Heidegger notes, engage today's reality. This seminar, with its seemingly specialized point of departure, in truth confronts the ultimate decisions that this reality compels us to take up.

For, if one attentively followed what emerged when we opposed the attempt to think of man on the basis of Da-sein against the philosophical determination of man as consciousness, it becomes clear that to the

surrender of the primacy of consciousness in favor of a new domain –
that of Dasein – there corresponds the fact that there is only one possibility for man to join this new domain: that of stepping into it, enter-
ing it, in order to stand in a relation to what is not man, in that man
receives his determination from there.

The entry into this domain is not produced by the thought undertaken by Heidegger. To believe thinking capable of changing the place
of man would still conceive of it on the model of production.

Therefore?

Therefore, let us say cautiously that thinking begins to prepare
the conditions for such an entry. In other words, Heidegger says, this
thinking above all prepares man for the possibility of corresponding to
such an entry.

III

Today's session, Saturday, September 8, 1973, opens with the reading of the protocol.

Heidegger first wishes to make a few additions to yesterday's work:

1) First with respect to what was said regarding the "imperatives":
in German, *"Zwang"* [imperative] belongs to *"zwingen"* (to necessitate,
to do violence to [to compel]).

This sociological or anthropological way of speaking, Heidegger
stresses, despite the undeniable results of the analyses it allows,[118]
nonetheless leaves the very notion of "imperative" undetermined in its
ontological character.

Now, I find the ontological determination of imperative, Heidegger
continues, in positionality [*Ge-stell*].

What is positionality? First, from a strictly linguistic point of view, it
has the following meanings:

In the *Ge-* one hears the gathering, the unification, the bringing together of all the modes of positing. Let us be more precise about the positing. Heidegger says: the meaning of positing is here that of a challenging. It is in this sense that one can say: "Nature is set upon [*hin gestellt*] to
yield energy" or: nature is compelled [*gezwungen*] to deliver its energy.
The meaning is that of a being *held to* something, whereby that which
is held to something is at the same time forced to adopt a certain form,
to play a role, a role to which it is henceforth reduced. Nature, held
to delivering its energy, henceforth appears as a "reserve of energy."

But, Heidegger immediately amends, as soon as nature is posed [*gestellt*] to deliver its energy, man is set [*gestellt*] to encounter and correspond
to these produced energies – to the extent that one can say: the greater
the challenging of nature, the greater the challenge man imposes on
himself. To give an example: coal, having become energy, then leads

to the discovery of oil as energy, which in turn leads to making nuclear energy available. One day, even nuclear energy will be succeeded.

Returning to the fundamental word positionality: It is a word with a striking form. In passing, and to avoid all ambiguity, it is to be noted that it could in no way designate, in Heidegger's usage, a simple matter [*bloße Sache*].

Its structure is indicative. There are words in German of the same type. Thus in Jakob Grimm, the word: *das Geschüh* (formed from *Schuh* [shoe]), which signifies "the wearing of shoes," "the cobbler's work," "footwear."

In his *Griechischen Kulturgeschichte*,[119] Jacob Burckhardt, speaking of the Athenians, indicates that they were largely governed by *das Gerühm* [glory] (formed from *Ruhm* [fame]). "*Das Gerühm*" thus means: everything that pertains to fame.

And in Gœthe we find, to name the haystacks in the streets of Palermo, *das Geströhde* (formed from *Stroh* [hay]).

Thus the word *das Ge-stell*, in the sense of a gathering of all the modes of *stellen* [positing], is linguistically possible.

Here a remark about the notion of *object*. For the scholastic word *objectum* is a translation of the Greek word: ἀντικείμενον. Would there be nevertheless something like an object in Greek?

This would mean neglecting the essential difference. Indeed, what does κεῖσθαι, the verb from which ἀντικείμενον derives, mean? It means: from itself, already lying before. Now it is characteristic of the *object* that, by means of representation, it is brought to a halt in an "over and against" [*im Gegenüber*]. It is representation that poses the object opposite it. The ἀντικείμενον already stands, that is, lies before – and from itself. The Greek experience does not yet require that representation play a role in the positing of a being. That beings *are*, the Greeks think this from out of φύσις – which Aristotle interprets from ποίησις as a bringing-forth into the open. One needs to distinguish from this Greek notion of *poiêsis* the modern notion of production, which means: to set into availability.

2) The second addendum bears on Marx.

The sentence cited yesterday – "To be radical is to grasp the root of the matter. But for man the root is man himself"[120] – that statement, Heidegger says, is not political, but metaphysical, which is clarified in the horizon of Feuerbach's reversal of Hegel's metaphysics. It can be seen in this way: for Hegel, the matter of knowledge is the Absolute in its dialectical becoming. Now Feuerbach reverses Hegel in making *man*, and no longer the Absolute, the matter of knowledge. In Marx's text, three lines after the cited passage, we read the following (which goes exactly in the direction of Feuerbach's critique): "The criticism of religion ends with the teaching that *man is the highest being for man.*"[121]

My Marx interpretation, Heidegger explains, is not political. It is concerned with being and the manner in which it destines itself. It is in this perspective and from this vision that I can say that with Marx the position of the most extreme nihilism is reached.[122]

This thesis does not mean anything other than: in the doctrine which explicitly states that *man* is the highest being for man, one finds the ultimate grounding and confirmation of the fact that being as being is *nothing* [*nihil*] anymore for man.

To understand Marx's statement politically is thus to make politics one of the modes of self-production–which is perfectly consistent with Marx's thought.

But how can we read this sentence otherwise, how can we read it as a metaphysical statement? By noting the strange *leap* made by Marx over a missing link. Indeed, what does the statement actually say?

"To be radical is to grasp the root of the matter. But for man the root is man himself." Here, Heidegger notes, an intermediary thought is missing, which makes it possible to go from the first thought to the second. *It is the idea that what matters* [die Sache] *is man.* For Marx, it is decided from the outset that man and only man (and nothing else) is what matters. From what is this decided? In what manner? With what right? By which authority?

One can only answer these questions by referring to the history of metaphysics. Marx's statement is thus decidedly to be understood as a metaphysical statement.

These additions made, we can return to the question that guides this entire seminar: the question concerning the access to being.

Heidegger speaks:

According to me, the entry into the essential domain of Da-sein, discussed at the end of yesterday's session–that entry which would render possible the experience of the instancy in the clearing of being–is only possible through the detour of a return to the beginning.

But this return is not a "return to Parmenides." It is not a question of returning *to* Parmenides. Nothing more is required than to *turn towards* Parmenides.

The return occurs in the echo of Parmenides. It occurs as that hearing which opens itself to the word of Parmenides from out of our present age, the epoch of the sending of being as positionality.

In *Being and Time*, there is already such a *return*, although still somewhat awkward. Indeed, in *Being and Time*, it takes place as destruction, that is, as disintegration, dismantling of that which, from the beginning, is destined as *being* in the uninterrupted succession of metamorphoses which is metaphysics.

But there was not yet in *Being and Time* a genuine knowledge of the history of being, hence the awkwardness and, strictly speaking, the naïveté of the "ontological destruction." Since then, this unavoidable naïveté of the novice gave way to a knowing.

To illustrate the question of the access to being, Heidegger proposes to read a text he wrote during winter 1972–1973. The theme of this text is the "heart of ἀλήθεια," of which Parmenides spoke. Heidegger explains that this theme resonates with that of Da-sein, for it is a question of the clearing itself. To a certain extent, it is a question of seeing how this showed itself to Parmenides. At the same time, Heidegger makes an essential correction in this text to what was said at the end of the lecture "The End of Philosophy and the Task of Thinking."[123] Opening to this passage, Heidegger reads:

"Or does it happen (that ἀλήθεια as clearing remains concealed) because self-concealing, concealment, Λήθη belongs to the Ἀ-λήθεια, not just as an addition, not as shadow to light, but rather as the heart of Ἀλήθεια?"

He explains: what is said here is not right; Parmenides says nothing of the sort.

It is thus a question of correctly listening to Parmenides. The text is entitled:

Ἀληθείης εὐκυκλέος ἀτρεμὲς ἦτορ

Heidegger reads slowly. What follows reconstitutes as much as possible the movement and articulation of the text as well as the commentaries that were given along with the reading. Ἀληθείη is translated as *Unverborgenheit [unconcealment]*. This translation is literal. As for what is named in this word, it has nothing yet to do with *truth;* it is important to emphasize this. On the contrary, here it all comes back to unconcealment, which indicates the There that man has to be.

Εὐκυκλέος is usually understood as "well-rounded," and is then taken as a quality of things.

But since here the word indicates ἀλήθεια, and since disclosure is not a thing, one cannot translate it in this way. Therefore it must be understood differently. To that end, we think εὔκυκλος as "that which encompasses well, the fitting encircling." Now ἀλήθεια is understood as what fittingly encircles. Ἀτρεμὲς ἦτορ: the untrembling heart. What is this? To discover it, we consider the first two verses of fragment 8:

"... there still remains just one saying of the path
which leads there, to the 'that it is' ..."

But precisely what is?

Patently, the being *is*, and not nothing. Thus this "that it is" (ὡς ἔστιν) would be τὰ ἐόντα (the being-together of all beings in a whole)? But in order to come to such a determination, there is no need—contrary to what Parmenides says—to take an unusual path. Something else is thus at issue. That the path is unusual indicates that what is at issue is what is most difficult to think. We are here in the situation of coming closer to being, just like Husserl with the notion of categorial intuition— but here it takes place in the echo of Parmenides, and not in an analysis of sensibility and the understanding, driven by a theory of knowledge. It concerns the "that it is." Our question, asked again, seeks to experience: *what* is? Parmenides's response is found in verse 1 of fragment 6:

ἔστι γὰρ εἶναι

not beings, but being. "Being namely *is*."

I have long considered this saying; for a long time, I have even been ensnared in it. For does it not reduce being to the level of beings? Only in regard to a being can one say that it is.

And here Parmenides now says: being *is*.

This unprecedented saying marks exactly the distance between ordinary thinking and the unusual path of Parmenides.

The question now is to know if we are capable of hearing with a Greek ear this Greek saying which speaks of ἔστι and εἶναι.

Thought in a Greek manner, εἶναι means to presence. It cannot be stressed enough how the Greek speaks so much *more revealingly* and thus more precisely than we do.

What is to be thought is thus: ἔστι γὰρ εἶναι—"presencing namely presences" [*anwest nämlich Anwesen*].

A new difficulty arises: this is clearly a tautology. Indeed! This is a genuine tautology: it names the Same only once, and indeed as itself.

We are here in the domain of the inapparent: presencing itself presences.

The name for what is addressed in this state of affairs is: τὸ ἐόν, which is neither beings, nor simply being, but τὸ ἐόν:

presencing: presencing itself [*Anwesend: Anwesen selbst*].

In this domain of the inapparent,[124] however (as verses 2 and 3 of fragment 8 state),

"along this path there are a great number of indications . . ."

Indication (σῆμα) must be understood here in the Greek sense: it is not something which stands as a "sign" for something else, but indication is what shows and lets be seen, in that it depicts what is to be seen.

In verse 29 of fragment 8, one finds just such an *indication*, which shows being:

Ταὐτόν τ᾽ ἐν ταυτῷ τε μένον καθ᾽ ἑαυτό τε κεῖται.

"The same dwelling in the same, it lies in itself."

This verse is itself εὔκυκλος, abundant and overflowing; it says on its own the complete tautology.

But a question is posed: Where and how does presence itself presence?

Answer: It presences in unconcealment. Thus, the non-trembling heart of ἀλήθεια is τὸ ἐόν itself!

Even this is also said by Parmenides. He actually names τὸ ἐόν, in verse 4 of fragment 8, ἀτρεμὲς.

The ἀλήθεια is no empty opening, no motionless chasm. One must think it as the disclosure which fittingly encircles the ἐόν, that is, the *presencing: presencing itself.*

Having thus answered the initial question, have we not as well arrived at the indemonstrable? Certainly. We must even assume that this is the only possible access both to the ἐόν and to ἀλήθεια. In any case, this is what Parmenides says, in fragment 1, verse 28:

"It is necessary that you experience all things."

Parmenides says here πυθέσθαι. It is not an ordinary experience, but authentic experience, the one spoken of in verse 1 of fragment 6:

"Saying (the letting-show-itself) and perceiving (what is accomplished with this) are necessary" —

Χρὴ τὸ λέγειν τε νοεῖν

This experience, and what it safeguards, is precisely what is said at the end of the same verse:

ἐόν ἔμμεναι — presencing presencing [*Anwesend Anwesen*].

This thought of Parmenides is neither judgment nor proof, nor a grounded explanation. It is rather a self-grounding upon what has let itself be seen.

As Goethe indicates, what is perhaps most difficult is to attain an unprejudiced observation. With Parmenides, this difficulty is precisely the issue: to hold in view *presencing: presencing.*

This itself, presencing-presencing, thoroughly attunes the fitting encircling unconcealment that discloses it.

Here ends the reading.

Heidegger continues: I name the thinking here in question tautological thinking. It is the primordial sense of phenomenology. Further, this kind of thinking is before any possible distinction between theory and praxis. To understand this, we need to learn to distinguish between *path* and *method*. In philosophy, there are only paths; in the sciences, on the contrary, there are only methods, that is, modes of procedure.

Thus understood, phenomenology is a path that leads away to come before. . . , and it lets that before which it is led show itself. This phenomenology is a phenomenology of the inapparent. Only now can one understand that there were no concepts for the Greeks. Indeed, in conceiving [*Be-greifen*], there is the gesture of taking possession. The Greek ὁρισμός on the contrary surrounds firmly and delicately that which sight takes into view; it does not con-ceive.

In the silence that follows, Jean Beaufret notes: The text we just heard completes, as it were, the long meditation in which you have turned first towards Parmenides and then Heraclitus. One could even say that your thinking has engaged differently with Heraclitus and Parmenides. Indeed, in *Vorträge und Aufsätze*, the primacy seemed to be given to Heraclitus. Today what place would Heraclitus take with respect to Parmenides?

Heidegger: From a mere historical perspective, Heraclitus signified the first step towards dialectic. From this perspective, then, Parmenides is more profound and essential (if it is the case that dialectic, as is said in *Being and Time*, is "a genuine philosophic embarrassment"[125]) In this regard, we must thoroughly recognize that tautology is the only possibility for thinking what dialectic can only veil.

However, if one is able to read Heraclitus on the basis of the Parmenidean tautology, he himself then appears in the closest vicinity to that same tautology, he himself then appears in the course of an exclusive approach presenting access to being.

Appendices

Appendix

German Translator's Afterword

I.

In the 1937 essay *"Wege zur Aussprache,"* Heidegger referred to France for the first time as the "neighbor people," with whom a "meditation to be achieved through productive reciprocal conversation"[126] would be historically necessary. This was explained through a reference to Leibniz, whose thinking was "constantly conducted in a confrontation with Descartes."[127] The "foundational and predetermining character of mathematical thinking in the principal sense" is indebted to the thinking of Descartes, i.e., to the "beginning of modern French philosophy," and from out of this grew the concept of nature for mathematical physics. Indeed, Heidegger sees the "meditation opened with respect to the essence of nature"—opened "predominantly through" Descartes and Leibniz—as "so little closed that it must be taken up once again on the basis of a more original posing of the question."[128] The question to be more originally posed is the one that Heidegger's own thinking sought to articulate, the clarification of which is the main concern of the *Four Seminars* as a whole, even if in 1966 this occurred for the most part indirectly. The statement following the previous citation makes clear what Heidegger already saw in 1937 as the task for thinking in France and Germany: "Only in this way do we also gain the preconditions for conceiving the metaphysical essence of technology, and thereby first achieve a conception of technology as a form for the installation of beings in one of their possible configurations."[129]

Even if it is only Descartes who is treated in the *Four Seminars* and not Leibniz's confrontation with him, nevertheless the recurrent thoughts on the age of modern technology along with the questions of the French participants concerning the essence of technology and the possibilities for the technological world all appear today as a peculiar echo of the citation from 1937. The early look to France also converges with the work recorded in these seminar protocols with French philosophers, poets, and scholars, in that the question concerning technology, though further elaborated and more pressingly formulated in the *Seminars,* remains underway and is not to be regarded as "closed."

The organization of the seminars themselves was such a manner of being underway. Heidegger explicitly related them to the condition where thoughtful meditation finds itself confronted by the essence of language that is required for the performance of action within the dominance of the technological world (see above, 51). In short, this is an essential part—though not the whole—of what these seminars meant for Heidegger.

In that same year of 1937, as the first French translations of his writings were already appearing, Heidegger received an invitation to France from the International Descartes Congress and the *Société française de philosophie,* with which, for various reasons, he did not follow through.[130] In "*Wege zur Aussprache,*" he had delimited "genuine philosophical self-understanding" from the "exchange of results in the sciences" which, "as is plain to see, must incessantly strive for a 'technologizing' and 'organization' (cf., for instance, the type and role of international congresses) in order to follow their long established path to its end. . . ."[131] Consequently, even though Heidegger certainly did not think congresses and similarly organized meetings to be the proper form for the necessary "reciprocal conversation of the creative ones in a neighborly encounter" — rather, 1937 called for a "writing which roots itself in such open discussions [*Aussprache*]"[132] — at that time, work groups like the *Four Seminars* were obviously not yet in view.

After the Second World War it was Jean Beaufret who did the most to motivate Heidegger's conversation with French thought. How this happened cannot be considered here in detail, especially since numerous other French intellectuals confronted Heidegger's thinking or attempted to take their start from him. It is to be recalled that already in his first letter to Jean Beaufret, a letter sent prior to the "Letter on Humanism," Heidegger had at that time made an early announcement of the seminars at hand — on November, 23, 1945, as the circumstances of the time would not allow for envisioning a meeting. As a supplement to the remarks on seminar work that are contained in the protocols, the following passage from a letter may be cited:

"Fruitful thinking requires not only writing and reading, but also the συνουσία of conversation and the work of learning-teaching. . . ."[133]

In the beginning, such work conversations took place in personal and individualized discussions.[134] With Heidegger's first trip to France in 1955 for the lecture "What is Philosophy?"[135] in Cerisy-la-Salle, he regretted that the trip did not lead to the seminar work he had intended. Indeed, in Paris at that time he met René Char whose stories of Provence called his attention to this landscape.[136] In 1956 and 1957 Heidegger took his first trips to Aix-en-Provence. In 1958 he held four lectures there; a comment in the French edition of the *Seminars* refers to it:

"After the lecture, 'Hegel and the Greeks,' held on March 20th, 1958 at the University of Aix-en-Provence, Heidegger made three further trips to Provence at the invitation of René Char. Thus came about the three seminars in Le Thor in 1966, 1968, and 1969."[137]

The *1966 Seminar* was not planned. The conversation begun by the mutual travelers led to the resolution that it be continued as a seminar. The theme was close to Heidegger, since he had agreed to participate in the Heraclitus-seminar of Eugen Fink in the coming winter semester at Freiburg.[138]

The sessions of the three seminars in Le Thor took place in the morning; afternoons were spent in common walks through the country with René Char (see below), but also in conversations and readings when all the participants visited him (René Char lived in L'Isle-sur-la-Sorgue, a few kilometers away from Le Thor). In 1966 Heidegger delivered the lecture "Hölderlin's Earth and Heaven."[139] He also prompted a conversation on Rimbaud. His question concerning Rimbaud's statement from his second letter about poetry (May 15, 1871)—*La Poésie ne rythmera plus l'action; elle* sera en avant—was eagerly answered by Char.[140] Heidegger took up the question of this sentence again in 1973, in a way connected with the endangerment of language discussed in the *Seminars*.[141]

Thus the "neighborliness" of the poet Char led to the seminars (he himself being present only in the last sitting of 1966) and also to conversations about poetizing and thinking. For Heidegger, these conversations and the seminars will have belonged together in many respects. In regard to this, the views on poetry given in the study hours and the dedication to the French translation of *On the Way to Language* all point to René Char (see below).

The *1968 Seminar* was prepared with greater consideration. Referring to his time in Marburg, Heidegger placed great weight on the work of a "model seminar." As in 1966 and 1969, all participants stayed in the same hotel, which provided a small hall for the study hours. In the afternoons, outings were taken once again and conversations and readings were likewise held. With Char, Heidegger read "The Poem,"[142] of which a French translation was also delivered.

The *1969 Seminar* was not originally foreseen, but conversations again soon led to it. The same division of the days was retained, morning work and afternoon excursions with René Char or visits with him. One afternoon, Heidegger read the poetry of Hölderlin with Char.

The extent to which Heidegger was occupied with the questions raised by the French participants can scarcely be more beautifully indicated than by a letter to Roger Munier written from Freiburg on July 31, 1969, before the beginning of the seminar and upon receipt of Munier's new translation of the lecture "What is Metaphysics?" The letter first concerns a retrospective look at the reception of the 1929 entrance lecture and the prospects of its question. In addition, taking his start from "What is Metaphysics?" and proceeding to the first of Munier's later questions taken up in the seminar (see above, 44–45), Heidegger states the only way that this further unfolded question of his thinking could be answered. The letter reads:

Dear Mr. Munier,
    First of all, I thank you for the new translation of my lecture 'What is Metaphysics?,' held forty years ago . . .

You probably know that this text, soon after its appearance (1929), was the first that was translated into the language of your country. Almost simultaneously, a Japanese translation appeared in 1930, composed by a young, highly gifted Japanese student who took part in my seminars.

The reaction to the piece in Europe was: nihilism and enmity to 'logic.' In the far East, with the 'nothing ' properly understood, one found in it the word for being.

In the course of the years, by means of a "Postscript" and an "Introduction," I attempted to clarify the text in regard to the return into the ground of metaphysics;[143] for "What is Metaphysics?" already pushed the question towards another dimension. There is no metaphysics of metaphysics. But this other dimension, from which metaphysics as such receives what is proper to it, is not yet determined even today. It remains difficult enough to enter into this determination as a task of thinking.

Your translation, which you present without any apparatus, requires our French friends and myself first of all to think through the matter of the lecture anew. This matter is a question. It places the very one who is questioning, and thus the Da-sein of the human, into question. It is important to experience Da-sein in the sense that man himself *is* the *"Da,"* i.e., the openness of being for him, in that he undertakes to preserve this and, in preserving it, to unfold it (Cf. *Being and Time*, p. 132 f.).

The matter of the lecture is a question. The answer sought, for its part as well, has the character of a question. The text ends with this question, and thus testifies to the finitude of thinking — or should we instead say: to the finitude of being, in the self-withdrawing manifestation of which the Da-sein of the human stands?

It is important to find in thinking what is thought-worthy for thinking, to endure it, and to experience it as what abides.

When we friends once again saw each other in September 1966 at the home of our mutual friend René Char in Provence, you gave me a text with seven questions. The first read: *Vous parlez, dans* Gelassenheit, *de la Puissance cachée dans la technique moderne. Qu'est-ce que cette Puissance, sur laquelle nous ne savons pas encore mettre de nom et qui ne procède pas de l'homme? Est-elle positive en son principe? Relève-t-elle de cette Contrée ouverte* (Gegnet) *où l'homme déploie librement son essence?*[144]

What you ask from the experience of modern technology's dominance is the same as what my lecture asked from the situation of science at that time.

Since then the interlocking of modern technology and modern science has become more poignant and more urgent. Today it appears to me to be equally the case that a sufficiently grounded insight into the relation of the two has not yet been gained.

I would still like to have the privilege one day of answering your seven questions, which I have continually reconsidered. Admittedly, this can occur only in the form of a more clarified question concerning the determination of thinking.

If I were able to unfold this question in an adequate manner, then I would voice the right thanks for the gift of your translation."[145]

For the *1973 Seminar*—named at the time the "Vosges-Seminar"[146]—
a gathering at the house of Roger Munier in the Vosges was originally
planned. It took place instead at Martin Heidegger's house in Zähringen, a region of Freiburg im Breisgau. The theme was, as the text says,
determined by the questions in a letter from Jean Beaufret. Concerning
the sort of expectations for this seminar, the following is excerpted from
a letter of Heidegger's to Roger Munier:

> Freiburg i. B. 16. IV. 73
>
> . . .
>
> In the past weeks, Beaufret, Fédier, and Vezin were here.
>
> I spoke with Fédier about the terminology and theme of the Vosges-
> Seminar. As a theme, there loomed before me: Husserl's VI Investigation
> from the *Logical Investigations*, more precisely the 2nd section, "Sense and
> Understanding," and from this: "categorial intuition." For me it is a mat-
> ter of actually performing an exercise in a phenomenology of the inap-
> parent; by the reading of books, no one ever arrives at phenomeno-
> logical "seeing."
>
> You can easily link this text to what particularly concerned you in my
> lecture *What Is Called Thinking?* It is my intent to experience ahead of
> time the passages which engage your questions. . . .

—In regard to this last seminar of Heidegger's, held outside the university, the participants came together in a free and friendly agreement.
Borne by Heidegger's untiring will to a "work of learning-teaching"—to
whose character as a thinker there belongs an ever-preparedness, or
even drive, to philosophical meditation—and likewise borne by the
passion of the French participants for his thinking, these seminars are
days of deep joy for those assembled. The acts and encounters must
have been attuned by a light friendliness. The recollections of a participant testify to this in a letter:

> It is actually impossible to reproduce the *mood* of these brilliant days:
> the reserved respect and admiration of the participants for Heidegger—
> they were all deeply permeated by the historical scope of this revolu-
> tionary thinking; but just as much by the relaxed, friendly, and close
> dealings with the teacher—in a word: the southern light, that is, the
> released joy of these unforgettable days.
>
> Heidegger and René Char saw each other every day. This often
> amounted to a visit, accompanied by Jean Beaufret or all the partici-
> pants, to Char's small house in Les Busclats. In the workshop of the poet
> or outdoors under the plane trees they conducted earnest and jovial
> conversations in a strikingly open sincerity.
>
> Daily we made splendid excursions with Heidegger in this country.
> Char led us to the most out-of-the-way and secret places. At time we
> came upon the blue Lubéron, which lay before us from out of
> Cézanne's[147] Provence, with the Montagne Sainte-Victoire in the dis-

tance. These were hours of the highest grace and happy emotion, the reflection of which was on the faces of everyone, even equally so on Heidegger's own.

The participants, all students of Jean Beaufret, mostly young and arriving here fresh from their studies, were greatly filled by a recognition of the pricelessness of what they took part in—and they attempted to give something of that back in return, by opening up a country, a face of the earth, to Heidegger's eyes and heart.

How strongly Heidegger's encounter with Provence entered into his thinking and how much the neighborly resonance of thinking and poetizing of these days delighted him, can be seen by the dedication and thoughtful composition to René Char that Heidegger inscribed in the French translation of *On the Way to Language.* The dedication reads:

"For
René Char
thankful for the nearness
of poetic dwelling
in the days of the seminar in Le Thor.
In friendly admiration
M.H."

On the back of the dedication, Heidegger set down words which present a short conversation between thinking and poetizing. He then closed with a question which can surely also be heard as a recollection of Hölderlin's travels through "southern France," which "familiarized him with the authentic essence of the Greeks" (Hölderlin named Provence in the hymn draft *"Vom Abgrund nemlich . . ."*[148]).

Worte von René Char, die uns die Nähe
des Dichtens und Denkens bezeugen:

Dans mon pays les tendres preuves
du printemps et les oiseaux mal habillés
sont préférés aux buts lointains.
. . . .
Dans mon pays, on remercie.
*
Avec celui que nous aimons, nous avons
cessé de parler, et ce n'est pas le silence.
L'éternité à Lourmarin Albert Camus.
*
La parole soulève plus de terre
que le fossoyeur ne le peut.
*
Ist die geliebte Provence die geheimnisvoll

unsichtbare Brücke vom frühen Gedanken
des Parmenides zum Gedicht Hölderlins?
M. H.[149]

II.

The basis of the translation is the text in Martin Heidegger, *Questions IV*, Paris: Gallimard, Classiques de la Philosophie, 1976.

The protocols of the seminars from 1966 stem exclusively from the preliminary remarks of Jean Beaufret. Apart from him, the participants were: Giorgio Agamben, Ginevra Bompiani, François Fédier, and François Vezin; for one session or a weekend: Dominique Fourcade and Roger Munier.

The protocols from 1968 first appeared under the title *Séminaire tenu par le Professeur Martin Heidegger sur la Differenzschrift de Hegel* in a 1969 printing (one hundred copies) arranged by Roger Munier for the seminar participants. They were collaboratively edited and, as in 1969, read by a participant in Heidegger's presence. The participants were: Jean Beaufret, François Fédier, François Vezin, Michel Deguy, Gérard Granel, Gofredo Iommi, Federico Camino, Jacques Bontemps, Giorgio Agamben, Patrick Lévy, and Michel Podgorny. Also taking part in one or two sessions: Roger Munier, Robert Davreu, Dominique Janicaud, and Pierre Badoual.

The seminar from 1969 appeared with the title *Séminaire tenu au Thor en septembre 1969 par le Professeur Martin Heidegger* in a printing meant for participants, likewise by Roger Munier, and without indication of year (two hundred copies). Editorial work and readings followed as in 1968. Those who took part: Jean Beaufret, François Fédier, François Vezin, Barbara Cassin, Patrick Lévy, Jean-François Grivas, and also for one or two sessions: Roger Munier, Julien Hervier, Robert Davreu, Franz Larese.

The texts of *Questions IV* are worked over; they often deviate from the private printings, though mostly only in form.

In 1973 the first protocol was drafted by Fédier and Vezin, the second by Mongis and Taminiaux, the third was tended to by Fédier, along with a final review of the whole. The first two were read in Heidegger's presence, who also read the final edition. Participants were: Jean Beaufret, François Fédier, François Vezin, Henri-Xavier Mongis, and Jacques Taminiaux.

In the German translation a few references and notes of the translator were added to the French protocol, the content of which were discussed with Heidegger. In regards to the typography, the guidelines for the *Collected Edition* of Heidegger's writings were observed, though the peculiarities of the French texts—such as the use of capital letters—were retained.

I heartily thank Jean Beaufret, François Fédier, and François Vezin for their help with the translation and for their information as to the details in the afterword. I thank Roger Munier for the friendly communication of the German text of Heidegger's letter.

Curd Ochwadt

Martin Heidegger, "The Provenance of Thinking"

The Provenance of Thinking

"From the Experience of Thinking" voices the thought:

> "We may venture the step back out of philosophy into the thinking of beyng as soon as we have become at home in the provenance of thinking" (1947).[150]

Are we already at home there? Hardly. What does it mean: to become at home in the provenance of thinking? It says: to attain a grounded residence in Dasein where thinking receives the determination of its essence.

Parmenides provides us with a first hint as to which way the provenance of thinking is to be questioned. This hint is contained in the claim:

> τὸ γὰρ αὐτὸ νοεῖν ἐστίν τε καὶ εἶναι (Fragment 3)
>
> "Thinking and being (i.e., perceiving and presencing) belong, namely, to one another."

Yet from where is this belonging to one another determined? What preserves here the possibility of this "to one another"?

For perception to be able to be encountered at all by the perceivable, it must hold itself open for . . . for what? For presencing [An-wesen]. Now for presencing to reign as such, it must be able to bring itself from itself into the open and the free dimension.

Both perception as well as presencing require for their own possibility — and this means at the same time for their "to one another" — a free and open dimension, within which they encounter one another.

And what is this? Parmenides names it Ἀλήθεια. It is to be experienced. More still. Not only it, but its "never trembling heart."

In order to become at home in the provenance of thinking, it is thus necessary to ponder what is named in the title of the following text.

This meditation is the precondition for sufficiently characterizing the "step back" and for being able to risk it with the required clarity; not as a doing of one's own, but rather from the compliance towards a call that is still held concealed in Ἀλήθεια itself and thus still remains reserved for thinking.

[The following text is equally an attempt to examine anew the earlier characterization of Ἀλήθεια in *On Time and Being*.[151]][152]

Martin Heidegger, "Parmenides: Ἀληθείης εὐκυκλέος ἀτρεμὲς ἦτορ"

"The well-rounded, unshaking heart of truth"—with these words from the "didactic poem" of Parmenides (Fragment I, 29), the Goddess names for the thinking man what he should experience in the course of his sojourn along the path that is first, both temporally and in terms of priority.

Before this, however, the Goddess characterizes the basic character of the whole journey in her greeting (Fragment I, 27):

ἦ γὰρ ἀπ' ἀνθρώπων ἐκτὸς πάτου ἐστίν·

"truly, it runs far away and outside the common residence of humans;"

This word of the Goddess still holds today, and probably more urgently so for every attempt to fittingly follow the originary thinking of Parmenides. Thus the common translation of the title words cited above probably also lacks the care of this demanding and unusual saying. It listens neither to the Greek language, nor does it bother with a precise and thoughtful determination of what is said by the Goddess. The truncated text at hand attempts to come nearer to such a determination.

The words of the Goddess read as a whole:

. . . χρεὼ δέ σε πάντα πυθέσθαι
ἠμὲν ἀληθείης εὐκυκλέος ἀτρεμὲς ἦτορ

". . . but it is necessary for you to experience everything [namely along all three of the paths to be pointed out by me] once [along the first, the main path], the well-rounded, never trembling heart of truth."

Ἀληθείη means, literally translated, unconcealment. Indeed, by means of such literalism even less is gained for an insight into the state of affairs thought by Parmenides. Ἀληθείη does not mean "truth," if what is meant by this is the validity of propositions in the form of statements. It is possible that what there is to think in ἀλήθεια, taken strictly for itself, has nothing yet to do with "truth," but everything to do with the unconcealment presupposed in every determination of "truth."

In order to make the disclosure that reigns in unconcealment more closely recognizable, let us keep to the epithet εὔκυκλος. It most commonly means "well rounded" as a property of things. Revealing, unconcealment, is nevertheless not a thing. We encounter its reign sooner, if we translate εὔκυκλος by "fitting encircling."

But Parmenides is supposed to experience along his first path not only this "fitting encircling unconcealment," but above all its ἀτρεμὲς ἦτορ, its "never trembling heart," that which everywhere pulses through all revealing, thoroughly attuning it, but which itself rests, lasts, and essences.

What is this? Does the Goddess tell us anything about it? Indeed; and poignantly enough, if we attend to what Parmenides finds before him, by her direction, upon his first path.

In Fragment VIII, 1 f., the Goddess says:

> . . . μόνος δ' ἔτι μῦθος ὁδοῖο
> λείπεται ὡς ἔστιν
>
> . . . "there still remains just one saying of the path that leads forth to there . . . (which shows): ὡς ἔστιν 'that it is';"

We are embarrassed and ask: What is, then? The answer lies near: it is obvious: beings and not nothing. But in order to establish such a thing, no unusual path beyond the ordinary representation and opinion of humans is required. It is much more a matter of bringing into view what is most difficult to think.

By his wording, Parmenides provides an unequivocal report concerning what the ὡς ἔστιν, "that it is," refers to. In Fragment VI, 1 he says: ἔστι γὰρ εἶναι, "[it] is: namely being." But in saying this, is not "being" mistaken for some being? Only of beings are we able to say "[it] is."

Before rushing to entrench ourselves in this objection, one which all too easily announces itself, we must first ask ourselves whether we also think in a Greek manner the Greek saying of the words: ἔστι and εἶναι; even more, whether we think something, on the whole, sufficiently determinate in our use of the words "is" and "being."

Thought in a Greek manner, εἶναι says: "to presence." This verb speaks more precisely. It brings us demonstrably closer to the matter to be thought. Accordingly, we must translate ἔστι γὰρ εἶναι as: "presencing namely presences" [*anwest nämlich anwesen*].

And—at the same time we come across a new difficulty. We stand before an obvious tautology. Certainly, and before a genuine one, too. It does not count the identical twice. Rather, it names the same, and it itself, once:

> ἔστιν εἶναι: "presencing (itself) presences"

According to Parmenides, the name for this state of affairs surrounding the matter of thinking is: τὸ ἐόν. This fundamental word of his thinking names neither "the being," nor merely "being." Τὸ ἐόν must be thought as a verbal participle. Then it says: "presencing: presencing itself" [*anwesend: anwesen selbst*]. Fragment VIII, 2 f. says of the only possible path of this saying:

. . . ταύτηι δ᾽ ἐπὶ σήματ᾽ ἔασι
πολλὰ μάλ᾽
"upon this, however, there are signs (showing)
indeed many;"

In regard to this showing, only one thing will be mentioned here. Verse 29 in Fragment VIII says of ἐόν:

ταὐτόν ἐν ταὐτῶι τε μένον καθ᾽ ἑαυτό τε κεῖται
"the same abiding in the same and resting in itself "

This verse provides a hint to the question which has been surreptitiously pressing upon us since the suggestion of thinking ἔστι and εἶναι, "presences" and "to presence," in a Greek manner. The question runs: Where and how does presencing presence [*west anwesen an*]? The answer: right "at" and in unconcealment. If this is apt, then the ἐόν, which alone is to be thought, is "the heart" of unconcealment. In verse 4 of Fr. VIII, Parmenides expressly names τὸ ἐόν: ἀτρεμές, "never trembling." Τὸ ἐόν, "resting in itself, thoroughly attunes and determines unconcealment."

Accordingly we cannot represent ἀληθείη as empty, rigid openness. Rather, we must think it as τὸ ἐόν, as "presencing: presencing itself" [*anwesend: anwesen selbst*], fitting, encircling revelation.

Indeed, with the preceding suppositions and questions are we not indulging in unprovable and hence arbitrary pronouncements concerning the relations between ἀλήθεια and ἐόν? Certainly—as long as we refrain from likewise thinking in a Greek manner the only possible type of access to each, the oft named "thinking," in which Parmenides moves.

In Fragment I, 28, the Goddess says:

. . . χρεὼ δέ σε πάντα πυθέσθαι
"It is necessary, however, for you to experience everything."

The required thinking is an experiencing, admittedly not ordinary sensual perception. The πυθέσθαι receives a closer determination at the corresponding passage (Fragment VI, 1):

χρὴ τὸ λέγειν τε νοεῖν τε . . .
"Saying [i.e., the letting show itself] and [the thus occuring] perceiving are necessary . . ." [to take up]

The thinking that here comes into play, far removed from common opinion, is: pure (non-sensuous) glimpsing [*Erblicken*]. What it has to glimpse is named conclusively in the same verse: ἐὸν ἔμμεναι: "presencing: presencing" [*anwesend: anwesen*].

This thinking is neither a judgment, nor a proof, nor a foundation. Rather, it grounds itself upon what was glimpsed.

To glimpse: "presencing itself presencing" — or not to glimpse, that is here — at the origin of Western thinking — the question.

Goethe writes ("Introduction to the *Propyläen*"):

> But who will not admit that unprejudiced observations [*reine Bemerkungen*] are rarer than is generally believed? We are so quick to mix our own fancies, opinions, judgements into what we experience. . .[153]

But first, how is one to glimpse τὸ ἐόν, the "presencing: presencing itself," if the observation is to keep itself free from prejudice?

"Observation" — an opportune word from the poet which at the same time attests that poets, "upon the most separated mountains," are near to the thinking of the thinkers.

The observation in the didactic-poem of Parmenides is now to be glimpsed:

> "That which presences: presencing itself thoroughly attunes
> the fitting revealing unconcealment, encircling it."

ἠμὲν Ἀληθείης εὐκυκλέος ἀτρεμὲς ἦτορ

On the Four Seminars

Heidegger gave the above mentioned manuscript of the Parmenides elucidation, including the preliminary remark "The Provenance of Thinking," to his brother Fritz on his eightieth birthday, "in memory of the years of mutual work." Since these texts belong together they are both presented here, though Heidegger did not deliver "The Provenance of Thinking" in the last session of the 1973 seminar. In conversation, Heidegger had considered placing the Parmenides elucidation at the place where it is recounted in the protocol. Since the preliminary remark cannot be inserted along with this text without falsifying the course of the seminar, the appendix now provides an acquaintance with the text as a whole, a text intended not solely for that seminar session. Further, the text was presented in the seminar with "elucidations . . . accompanying the reading," which are entered into the protocol. For this reason as well, the text of the protocol remains unaltered. In comparing the two, along with repetitions, one finds conclusions drawn from the elucidations.

On August 30, 1968, Heidegger delivered the self-made abridgment — "A torn sock is better than a mended one" — as an early note of Hegel's that was familiar to him for years. He had used that very passage in the lecture course *What Is Called Thinking?* and during its printing either he or an editorial assistant had replaced it with the original text as presented by Rosenkranz.[154] In Le Thor, François Vezin recalled this formulation of Hegel's text, which Heidegger explained at the time as a "correction" by the "printer." If no misunderstanding arose here in the bilingually held session, it would be obvious that the printer's acting proofreader, in French *prote*, was meant. Otto Pöggeler imparted in 1978 that "printer" could refer back to an erroneous recollection of a conversation in the Hegel Archive about the printing history of Hegel's "Wastebook,"[155] which took place in the early summer of 1964 as Heidegger visited the archive. I see no other explanation.

Heidegger cites Hegel's wording in *Off the Beaten Track;*[156] so Heidegger would have retained "Hegel's" version more than once. Heidegger's formulation probably appealed to him due to the pleasure he took in the raw imagery of Hegel's words, even carrying it too far. It should provide us with an indication of his intensive engagement with Hegel's language. We should not explain away Heidegger's own coinage as simply false — we would instead, perhaps, offer the reproach that Hegel makes to his contemporary "would-be philosophers," that they are "letter-bound men."[157] Hegel's *thought* — the fact that what is torn and thus "open to admit the absolute,"[158] is "better" than the "mended consciousness" of everyday self-satisfaction — is retained in Heidegger's formulation. It changes nothing that the 1968 citation is, in the first place, only for an "exercise in phenomenological kindergarten." Both times, in 1952 and in 1968, delivered *without* the additional phrase, the passage says the same as Hegel's note *with* the additional phrase, even if it does not agree with it *literally*. In 1952, Heidegger was prompted by a number of those listening to move from the "tear of consciousness" to the self-satisfied "mended consciousness," a fact mentioned in the notes of the editor, since it was not entered into the printed protocol. Twice the audience laughed over the "torn sock" saying. At first Heidegger answered pedantically, "I do not know why you are laughing. You must learn to endure the scope of a sentence such as the one I have cited." Wishing to continue and repeating the saying, but once again being met with laughter, Heidegger reacted in angered disappointment: "Perhaps you all live with a mended consciousness." — Heidegger's coining first becomes false if the additional phrase is appended, and only insofar as the "tear" would then be denied to self-consciousness.

Endnotes to the Translation

1. See pp. 85–92.

2. As Heidegger refers to the French in the 1937 essay *"Wege zur Aussprache,"* pp. 15–21 in Martin Heidegger, *Aus der Erfahrung des Denkens*, ed. Hermann Heidegger (Frankfurt am Main: Vittorio Klostermann, 1983), p. 15; Vol. 13 of Martin Heidegger, *Gesamtausgabe*, 102 vols. to date, gen. ed. Friedrich-Wilhelm von Herrmann (Frankfurt am Main: Vittorio Klostermann, 1977–), hereafter cited as GA.

3. Martin Heidegger and Imma von Bodmershof, *Briefwechsel 1959-1976*, ed. Bruno Pieger (Stuttgart: Klett-Cotta, 2000) p. 83.

4. See the German translator's afterword, pp. 90–91.

5. On the unique relation between Heidegger and France, the reader is referred to the work of Dominique Janicaud on the history of the French reception of Heidegger. His two volume *Heidegger en France* (Paris: Albin Michel, 1991) is a momentous and exhaustive survey of this rich terrain. Both translators have benefited from the conversation and friendship of Professor Janicaud, an attendee of these very seminars, throughout the years. We mourn his recent and untimely passing.

6. For the German text: Martin Heidegger, *Vier Seminare*, trans. Curd Ochwadt (Frankfurt am Main: Vittorio Klostermann, 1977), now pp. 267–421 of Martin Heidegger, *Seminare*, GA 15, ed. Curd Ochwadt, 1986. For the French text: Martin Heidegger, *Questions IV* (Paris: Gallimard, 1976), pp. 195–339.

7. Information provided on the jacket of the first German edition of *Vier Seminare:*

> During his lifetime, Martin Heidegger stood in a close relation to France. The path to numerous encounters with philosophers, poets, and painters in Paris and the south of France was paved by Jean Beaufret, to whom Heidegger had addressed the 1947 "Letter on Humanism."
>
> Four seminars that Heidegger held with seven French scholars and the poet René Char were transcribed as protocol and (after the French edition) now appear in a German translation monitored by Heidegger.

8. See Ochwadt's editorial afterward to GA 15, p. 441.

9. Martin Heidegger, *Contributions to Philosophy (from Enowning)*, trans. Parvis Emad and Kenneth Maly (Bloomington, Ind.: Indiana University Press, 1999). German text: Martin Heidegger, *Beiträge zur Philosophie (vom Ereignis)*, GA 65, ed. Friedrich-Wilhelm von Herrmann, 1989.

10. Martin Heidegger, *Prolegomena zur Geschichte des Zeitbegriffs*, GA 20, 3d ed., ed. Petra Jaeger, 1994. English translation: Martin Heidegger, *History of the Concept of Time: Prolegomena*, trans. Theodore Kisiel (Bloomington: Indiana University Press, 1985).

11. Martin Heidegger, *"Andenken an Marcelle Mathieu,"* pp. 731–732 of Martin Heidegger, *Reden und andere Zeugnisse eines Lebensweges*, GA 16, ed. Hermann Heidegger, 2000, p. 731.

12. René Char, *Œuvres complètes*, (Paris: Gallimard, 1983), p. 452. A translation:

To M.H.
(Martin Heidegger)
Autumn moves back and forth faster than
the gardener's rake. Autumn does not assail
the heart that requires the branch with its shadow.

Les Busclats: cf. p. 89.

TN: The single edition of *Vier Seminare* supplies the following: The poem by René Char first appeared in: *Dans la pluie giboyeuse* (Paris: Gallimard, 1968), p. 21. Later also in: *Le nu perdu* (Paris: Gallimard, 1971), p. 67.

13. René Char, *Commune Présence* (Paris: Gallimard, 1964), p. 72.

14. Aristotle, *Rhetoric*, trans. W. Rhys Roberts, in Aristotle, *The Complete Works of Aristotle*, 2 Vols., trans. various, ed. Jonathan Barnes (Princeton: Princeton University Press, 1995), Vol. 2: 2152–2269; Book 3: 5. TN: The German edition of the text mistakenly refers to *Rhetoric* Book 2: 5. We are indebted to Prof. Dr. Heinrich Hüni for this correction.

15. Hermann Diels, trans., Walther Kranz, ed., *Die Fragmente der Vorsokratiker*, 6th ed., 3 Vols. (Zürich: Weidmann, 1951). Hereafter cited as "DK."

16. Martin Heidegger, *Der Satz vom Grund* (Pfullingen: Verlag Günther Neske, 1957), pp. 177, 179, 182. English translation: Martin Heidegger, *The Principle of Reason*, trans. Reginald Lily (Bloomington: Indiana University Press, 1991), pp. 106, translation modified (hereafter: tm), 107, 109.

17. Martin Heidegger, *Sein und Zeit*, 17th ed. (Tübingen: Max Niemeyer Verlag, 1993). English translation: *Being and Time*, trans. John Macquarrie and Edward Robinson (San Francisco: Harper & Row, Publishers, 1962), pp. 175f. TN: Page references will be to the German text, the pagination of which is reproduced marginally in the English translation.

18. TN: The French reads: "*Héraclite n'est pas encore* xénophobe *au sens de Platon.*" In English: "Heraclitus is not yet *xenophobic* in Plato's sense."

19. Martin Heidegger and Eugen Fink, *Heraklit*, ed. Friedrich-Wilhelm von Herrmann (Frankfurt am Main: Vittorio Klostermann, 1970), pp. 179f. English translation: Martin Heidegger and Eugen Fink, *Heraclitus Seminar*, trans. Charles H. Seibert (Evanston: Northwestern University Press, 1993), p. 112.

20. R. Char, *Commune Présence*, p. 129.

21. Hesiod, *Theogony*, pp. 78–155 in *Hesiod. Homeric Hymns. Epic Cycle. Homerica*, ed. and trans. Hugh G. Evelyn-White (Cambridge: Harvard University Press, 2000), 133, tm.

22. TN: *abkehren*, the French text reads "*dif-férent.*"

23. Cf. Martin Heidegger, *Nietzsche*, 2 Vols. (Pfullingen: Verlag Günther Neske, 1961), vol. 1, 599. English translation in: Martin Heidegger, *The Will to Power as Knowledge and as Metaphysics*, trans. David Farrell Krell, Frank A. Capuzzi, and Joan Stambaugh (San Francisco: Harper & Row, 1987), pp. 107–108, vol. 3 of Martin Heidegger, *Nietzsche*, 4 Vols., trans. various, ed. David Farrell Krell (San Francisco: Harper & Row, Publishers, 1979–1987).

24. Tristan L'Hermite, "*Le promenoir des deux amants,*" ll. 3–4, from the collection *Les Amours de Tristan* (1638), in Tristan L'Hermite, *Œuvres complètes*, vol. 2: *Poésie (I)*, ed. Jean-Pierre Chauveau (Paris: Honoré Champion, 2002), p. 105.

25. Aeschylus, *The Libation Bearers*, trans. Richmond Lattimore, in vol. 1 of *The Complete Greek Tragedies*, 4 Vols., eds. David Grene and Richmond Lattimore, trans. various (Chicago: University of Chicago Press, 1992), p. 319.

26. Martin Heidegger, *"Der Feldweg,"* in GA 13: 87–90, p. 90. English translation: "The Pathway," trans. Thomas F. O'Meara, revised by Thomas J. Sheehan, *Listening* 8 (1973): 32–39.

27. The Char citation adopted as epigraph indicates what thinking in the beginning ("morning") of Western history had "first" found: the question of metaphysics.

28. Title of the René Char collection *À la santé du serpent* (Paris: Gallimard, 1954).

29. Georges Braque, *Le jour et la nuit: Cahiers 1917–1952* (Paris: Gallimard, 1952), pp. 26, 30.

30. Cf. Martin Heidegger and Eugen Fink, *Heraklit,* pp. 93–112. *Heraclitus Seminar,* pp. 56–67.

31. Originally the title of a poem in the collection *Le marteau sans maître* (Paris: José Corti, 1945). See 1, note 13.

32. Hermann Diels, *Parmenides* (Berlin: G. Reimer, 1897), p. 66.

33. Nietzsche, "Preface to Richard Wagner," *The Birth of Tragedy,* trans. Walter Kaufmann (New York: Vintage Books, 1967), p. 31.

34. René Char, *La parole en archipel* (Paris: Gallimard, 1962), p. 119. The "ones who belong to each other" named by Char (*Les Attenants*) were familiar to Hölderlin, as when, for example, he says:

> "But rock needs splitting,
> Earth needs furrowing . . ."

(from Friedrich Hölderlin, "The Ister" (lines 68–69), in Friedrich Hölderlin, *Gedichte nach 1800,* ed. Friedrich Beißner (Stuttgart: W. Kohlhammer, 1951), p. 192, vol. 2.1 of Friedrich Hölderlin, *Sämtliche Werke,* Grosse Stuttgarter Ausgabe, 8 Vols., gen. ed. Friedrich Beißner (Stuttgart: W. Kohlhammer, 1946–1985), hereafter cited as GSA. English translation in: Friedrich Hölderlin, *Hymns and Fragments,* trans. Richard Sieburth (Princeton, N.J.: Princeton University Press, 1984), p. 115, "fissures" and "rock," "furrows" and "earth" are "ones who belong to each other" in Char's sense, which means in Greek: ἀλλήλων ἐχόμενα.

35. Martin Heidegger, *Aus der Erfahrung des Denkens,* in GA 13: 80. English translation in: Martin Heidegger, *Poetry, Language, Thought,* trans. Albert Hofstadter (New York: Harper & Row, Publishers, 1971), p. 8.

36. "Losing the site": cf. *Einführung in die Metaphysik* 4th ed. (Tübingen: Max Niemeyer Verlag, 1976), p. 113. English translation: Martin Heidegger, *Introduction to Metaphysics,* trans. Gregory Fried and Richard Polt (New Haven: Yale University Press, 2000), p. 157. "Well deserving [indeed]": cf. the lecture " . . . poetically man dwells. . . ," in Martin Heidegger, *Vorträge und Aufsätze,* 7th ed. (Stuttgart: Verlag Günther Neske, 1994), pp. 181–198. English translation in: Martin Heidegger, *Poetry, Language, Thought,* pp. 211–229.

37. G. W. F. Hegel, *Differenz des Fichte'schen und Schelling'schen Systems der Philosophie,* (Hamburg: Meiner Verlag (Philos. Bibl. 62a), 1962). TN: English translation: G. W. F. Hegel, *The Difference Between Fichte's and Schelling's System of Philosophy,* trans. H. S. Harris and Walter Cerf (Albany: State University of New York Press, 1977). Parenthetical references within the seminar to Hegel's text (hereafter *"Differenzschrift"*) will first refer to Heidegger's German edition with the English translation following after a slash.

38. J. G. Fichte, *Briefwechsel.* 2 Vols. Ed. Hans Schultz. 2nd expanded edition (Leipzig: H. Haessel, 1930), 2: 340.

39. TN: Heidegger's citation differs from the published one, which reads in full, "A mended sock is better than a torn one; not so with self-consciousness." See G. W. F. Hegel, *Werke*, ed. Eva Moldenhauer and Karl Markus Michel, vol. 2: *Jenaer Schriften, 1801–1807* (Frankfurt: Suhrkamp Verlag, 1970), p. 558. English translation in: G. W. F. Hegel, "Aphorisms from the Wastebook," trans. Susanne Klein et al., *Independent Journal of Philosophy* Vol. 3 (1976): 1–6, p. 4. On the surrounding controversy, see the German editor's afterword, pp. 98–99.

40. TN: As Heidegger will often return to this and the surrounding passages from the section "The Need of Philosophy" in the *Differenzschrift*, these passages are here provided as a whole:

> Opposites such as spirit and matter, soul and body, faith and understanding, freedom and necessity, etc. used to be important; and in more limited spheres they appeared in a variety of other guises. The whole weight of human interests hung upon them. With the progress of culture they have passed over into such forms as the opposition of Reason and sensibility, intelligence and nature and, with respect to the universal concept, of absolute subjectivity and absolute objectivity.
>
> The sole interest of Reason is to sublate such rigid opposites. But this does not mean [14] that Reason is altogether opposed to opposition and limitation. For the necessary dichotomy is One factor in life. Life eternally forms itself by setting up oppositions, and totality at the highest pitch of living energy is only possible through its own re-establishment out of the deepest fission. What Reason opposes, rather, is just the absolute fixity which the understanding gives to the dichotomy; and it does so all the more if the absolute opposites themselves originated in Reason.
>
> When the power of conjoining vanishes from the life of men and the opposites lose their living connection and reciprocity and gain independence, the need of philosophy arises.
>
> [*Differenzschrift*, 13–14/90–91; tm]

41. "*Selbstbewusstsein*" here would not have the philosophical sense of self-consciousness, but the common sense it has in ordinary language: arrogance or pretension: "Everyday experience thinks otherwise," Heidegger says by way of clarification. TN: Note deleted in *Gesamtausgabe* version of the *Seminars*.

42. Or, starting from Hegel's sentence: natural consciousness in the "mended condition" of an essentially torn constitution of self-consciousness; as such not even glimpsed by natural consciousness. TN: German translator's note added to the *Gesamtausgabe* version of the *Seminars*.

43. Cf. GA 5: 144 *Off the Beaten Track*, ed. and trans. Julian Young and Kenneth Haynes (Cambridge: Cambridge Univesity Press, 2002), p. 108. TN: Note added to the *Gesamtausgabe* version of the *Seminars*.

44. TN: emphasis added in protocol; translation slightly modified.

45. Edmund Husserl, *The Crisis of European Sciences and Transcendental Phenomenology: An Introduction to Phenomenological Philosophy*, trans. David Carr (Evanston, Ill.: Northwestern University Press, 1970).

46. TN: As Sunday is not a typical workday, the term "Sunday seminar" refers to a seminar conducted in a more informal manner than one would expect from a "workday" seminar.

47. Words uttered September 2.

48. Immanuel Kant, *Critique of Pure Reason*, trans. Norman Kemp Smith (New York: St. Martin's Press, 1965), A 613/B 641.

49. TN: Heidegger's analysis will largely focus on the closing paragraphs of the section entitled "The Need of Philosophy" and the opening paragraphs of the following section "Reflection as Instrument of Philosophizing." These paragraphs are reproduced here in their textual order:

> In the struggle of the understanding with Reason the understanding has strength only to the degree that Reason foresakes itself. Its success in the struggle therefore depends upon Reason itself, and upon the authenticity of the need for the reconstitution of the totality, the need from which Reason emerges.
>
> The need of philosophy can be called the *presupposition* of philosophy if philosophy, which begins with itself, has to be furnished with some sort of vestibule; and there has been much talk nowadays about an absolute presupposition. What is called the presupposition of philosophy is nothing else but the need that has come to utterance. Once uttered, the need is posited for reflection, so that [because of the very nature of reflection] there must be two presuppositions.
>
> One is the Absolute itself. It is the goal that is being sought; but it is already present [*vorhanden*], or how otherwise could it be sought? Reason produces it, merely by freeing consciousness from its limitations. This sublation of the limitations is conditioned by the presupposed unlimitedness.
>
> The other presupposition may be taken to be that consciousness has stepped out of the totality, that is, it may be taken to be the split into being and not-being, concept and being, finitude and infinity. From the standpoint of the dichotomy, the absolute synthesis is a beyond, it is the undetermined and the shapeless as opposed to the determinacies of the dichotomy. The Absolute is the night, and the light is younger than it; and the distinction between them, like the emergence of the light out of the night, is an absolute difference—the nothing is the first out of which all being, all the manifoldness of the finite has emerged. The task of philosophy, however, consists in uniting these presuppositions: to posit being in non-being, as becoming; to posit dichotomy in the Absolute, as its appearance; to posit the finite in the infinite, as life.
>
> It is clumsy, however, to express the need of philosophy as a presupposition of philosophy, for the need acquires in this way a reflective form. This reflective form appears as contradictory statements, which we shall discuss below. One may require of statements that they [17] be justified. But the justification of these statements as presuppositions is still not supposed to be philosophy itself, so that the founding and grounding gets going before, and outside of, philosophy.
>
> REFLECTION AS INSTRUMENT OF PHILOSOPHIZING
>
> The form that the need of philosophy would assume, if it were to be expressed as a presupposition, allows for a transition from the need of philosophy to the *instrument of philosophizing*, to *reflection* as Reason. The task of philosophy is to construct the Absolute for consciousness. But since the

productive activity of reflection is, like its products, mere limitation, this task involves a contradiction. The Absolute is to be posited in reflection. But then it is not posited, but sublated; for in having been posited it was limited [by its opposite]. Philosophical reflection is the mediation of this contradiction. What must be shown above all is how far reflection is capable of grasping the Absolute, and how far in its speculative activity it carries with it the necessity and possibility of being synthesized with absolute intuition. To what extent can reflection be as complete for itself, subjectively, as its product must be, which is constructed in consciousness as the Absolute that is both conscious and non-conscious at the same time?

Reflection in isolation is the positing of opposites, and this would be a sublation of the Absolute, reflection being the faculty of being and limitation. But reflection as Reason has connection with the Absolute, and it is Reason only because of this connection. In this respect, reflection nullifies itself and all being and everything limited, because it connects them with the Absolute. But at the same time the limited gains standing precisely on account of its connection with the Absolute.

[*Differenzschrift*, 16-17/93-94; tm]

50. TN: *Differenzschrift*, 16/93; tm.
51. TN: *Differenzschrift*, 16/94; tm.
52. TN: *Differenzschrift*, 17/94; tm.
53. TN: *Differenzschrift*, 17/94; tm.
54. TN: In full, "The need of philosophy can appease itself by simply penetrating to the principle of nullifying all fixed opposition and connecting the limited to the Absolute. This appeasement found in the principle of absolute identity is characteristic of philosophy as such" (33/112, tm).
55. TN: Kant, *Critique of Pure Reason*, B 131.
56. Augustine, *St. Augustine's Confessions*, 2 Vols., trans. William Watts (Cambridge: Harvard University Press, 1912), Vol. I, Bk. 8, ch. 12. TN: From the scene of Augustine's conversion, "take up and read."
57. Kant, *Critique of Pure Reason*, B xxx.
58. Playing on a French joke according to which the dullness of cattle expresses itself in hour-long "gaping" at the trains travelling by.
59. TN: See, for example, the *Economic and Philosophic Manuscripts of 1844*, "Private Property and Communism," where one can read: "We have seen how on the assumption of positively annulled private property man produces man—himself and the other man; how the object, being the direct manifestation of his individuality, is simultaneously his own existence for the other man, the existence of the other man, and that existence for him. [. . .] *just as* society itself produces *man as man*, so is society *produced* by him." Karl Marx and Friedrich Engels, *Economic and Philosophic Manuscripts of 1844*, trans. Martin Milligan, pp. 297-298, in *Marx and Engels: 1843-1844*, trans. various, vol. 3 of Karl Marx and Friedrich Engels, *Collected Works*, 49 vols., ed. Jack Cohen et al. (New York: International Publishers; London: Lawrence & Wishart; Moscow: Progress Publishers, 1975-2001), hereafter cited as "CW."
60. Kant, *Critique of Pure Reason*, B 358, B 875.
61. On the systematic, see again Kant, *Critique of Pure Reason*, A 645, B 673.
62. TN: See note 49, above.

63. "The Absolute is to be reflected [*soll reflektiert . . . werden*]": "*Sollen*" indicates here "the task of philosophy." Hegel says: "The task of philosophy is to construct the Absolute for consciousness. but since the productive activity of reflection is, like its products, mere limitation, this task involves a contradiction" (*Differenzschrift*, 17/94).

64. TN: See note 49, above.

65. TN: Heidegger is referring, somewhat mistakenly, to the opening proposition of Wittgenstein's *Tractatus Logico-Philosophicus*, "The world is all that is the case" (Ludwig Wittgenstein, *Tractatus Logico-Philosophicus*, trans. D. F. Pears and B. F. McGuinness (New York: Routledge, 2001), proposition 1, p. 5). But insofar as Wittgenstein understands the world as "the sum-total of reality" (proposition 2.063; p. 9), Heidegger's claim is true to the text.

66. Mountain range near Le Thor.

67. TN: Heidegger is referring to the passage at the opening of Descartes's second *Meditation*, where Descartes compares his project to that of Archimedes, claiming that "Archimedes used to demand just one firm and immovable point [*firmum & immobile*] in order to shift the entire earth; so I too can hope for great things if I manage to find just one thing, however slight, that is certain and unshakeable [*quod certum sit & inconcussum*]. René Descartes, *Meditationes de Prima Philosophia*, vol. 7 of René Descartes, *Œuvres de Descartes*, 12 vols., ed. Charles Adam and Paul Tannery (Paris: J. Vrin, 1964–1976), p. 24. English translation: René Descartes, *Meditations on First Philosophy*, in vol. 2 of René Descartes, *The Philosophical Writings of Descartes*, 3 vols., ed. and trans. John Cottingham, Robert Stoothoff, and Dugald Murdoch (Cambridge: Cambridge University Press, 1984–1991), p.16.

68. Hölderlin's second letter to Böhlendorf. Friedrich Hölderlin, GSA 6.1: *Briefe*, ed. Adolf Beck, 1954, "Letter Nr. 240: An Casimir Ulrich Böhlendorf," pp. 432–433. English translation in: Friedrich Hölderlin, *Friedrich Hölderlin: Essays and Letters on Theory*, trans. and ed. Thomas Pfau (Albany: State University of New York Press, 1988), pp. 152–153.

69. Cf. Plato, *Theaetetus*, trans. M. J. Levett, rev. Myles Burnyeat, in Plato, *Complete Works*, ed. John M. Cooper (Indianapolis: Hackett Publishing Company, 1997), 155d.

70. Friedrich Nietzsche, *Twilight of the Idols*, in *The Portable Nietzsche*, ed. and trans. Walter Kaufmann (New York: Viking Penguin Inc., 1982), pp. 485–486.

71. Cf. Aristotle, *Metaphysics*, trans. W. D. Ross, in Aristotle, *The Complete Works of Aristotle*, vol. 2: 1552–1728; Bk. Z, 1041 a 1–3.

72. Cf. Martin Heidegger, *Being and Time*, p. 143.

73. TN: Martin Heidegger, "*Aus der Erfahrung des Denkens*," now in GA 13: 75–86. English translation: "The Thinker as Poet," pp. 1–14 in Martin Heidegger, *Poetry, Language, Thought*. For "topology of beyng," see 84/12, tm. Martin Heidegger, "*Die Kunst und der Raum*," now in GA 13: 203–210. English translation: Martin Heidegger, "Art and Space," trans. Charles H. Seibert, *Man and World* 6 (1973):3–8.

74. Martin Heidegger, "Hegel and the Greeks," in Martin Heidegger, *Wegmarken*, 2d ed., GA 9, ed. Friedrich-Wilhelm von Herrmann, 1996, p. 443. English translation: Martin Heidegger, *Pathmarks*, trans. various, ed. William McNeill (Cambridge: Cambridge University Press, 1998), pp. 334–335.

75. Cited in Henri Mondor, *Vie de Mallarmé* (Paris: Gallimard, 1946), p. 683.

76. In the course of the 1966 seminar in Le Thor.

77. Martin Heidegger, *Gelassenheit* (Pfullingen: Verlag Günther Neske, 1959), p. 18. English translation: Martin Heidegger, *Discourse on Thinking*, trans. John M. Anderson and E. Hans Freund (New York: Harper & Row, 1966), p. 50.

78. Martin Heidegger, *Gelassenheit*, p. 19/*Discourse on Thinking*, p. 51.

79. Martin Heidegger, *Hebel der Hausfreund*, GA 13: 133–150, p. 146. English translation: "Hebel — Friend of the House," trans. Bruce V. Foltz and Michael Heim, *Contemporary German Philosophy* (University Park: Pennsylvania State University Press), Vol. 3 (1984):89–101, p. 98.

80. GA 13: 146/"Hebel — Friend of the House," p. 98.

81. Martin Heidegger, *Gelassenheit*, p. 23/*Discourse on Thinking*, p. 54.

82. Martin Heidegger, *Gelassenheit*, p. 24/*Discourse on Thinking*, p. 55.

83. "Kant's Thesis About Being," in GA 9: 445–480/*Pathmarks*, pp. 337–363.

84. Immanuel Kant, *Metaphysical Foundations of Natural Science*, trans. James W. Ellington (Indianapolis: Hackett Publishing Company, 1985), pp. 3–17.

85. TN: "Nothing is more proper to emergence than concealment." Or better: "Nothing is more *dear* to emergence than concealment."

86. TN: Edmund Husserl, *Logical Investigations*, 2 Vols., trans. J. N. Findlay (Atlantic Highlands, N. J.: Humanities Press, Inc., 1982). See Investigation 1, chapter 1, section 9, "Phenomenological distinctions between the phenomena of physical expression and the sense-giving and sense-fulfilling act."

87. G. W. F. Hegel, *Hegel's Science of Logic*, trans. A. V. Miller (Atlantic Highlands, NJ: Humanities Press International, Inc., 1969), p. 82; First book, first section, first chapter, C1.

88. TN: Martin Heidegger, "What Is Metaphysics?" in GA 9: 103–122/*Pathmarks*, pp. 82–96.

89. TN: Martin Heidegger, "*Der Weg zur Sprache*," in Martin Heidegger, *Unterwegs zur Sprache*, 10th ed. (Stuttgart: Verlag Günther Neske, 1993), pp. 267–268. English translation: "The Way to Language," in Martin Heidegger, *On the Way to Language*, trans. Peter D. Hertz (San Francisco: Harper & Row, 1971), p. 136.

90. Karl Marx, "Theses on Feuerbach," trans. Clemens Dutt, in Karl Marx and Friedrich Engels, *Marx and Engels: 1845–47*, trans. various, CW5, p.8. On thesis 11, cf. "Kant's Thesis About Being" in GA 9: 446–447/*Pathmarks*, p. 338.

91. "Without Hegel, Marx would not have been able to transform the world," says Heidegger emphatically.

92. Aristotle, *Nicomachean Ethics*, trans. W. D. Ross, revised by J. O. Urmson, in *The Complete Works of Aristotle*, Vol. 2: 1729–1867; Book 10: 5–6.

93. Aristotle, *Physics*, trans. R. P. Hardie and R. K. Gaye, in *The Complete Works of Aristotle*, Vol. 1: 315–446; Book 3: 1, 201a 10–11.

94. TN: A reference to the concluding "General Scholium" of Newton's *The Principia: Mathematical Principles of Natural Philosophy*, trans. I. Bernard Cohen and Anne Whitman (Berkeley: University of California Press, 1999), p. 943.

95. Kant, *Critique of Pure Reason*, A 189.

96. TN: Beaufret's reference is not a direct citation, as one may be led to believe from the reference provided by the German text. Instead, Beaufret's remark recapitulates developments found on pages 26–27 of the essay "The Question Concerning Technology," in *Vorträge und Aufsätze* 7th ed. (Stuttgart: Verlag Günther Neske, 1994), English translation in Martin Heidegger, *The Question Concerning Technology and Other Essays*, trans. William Lovitt (New York: Harper & Row, 1977), p. 23, tm:

Hence physics, in all its retreating from the representation turned only toward objects that has alone been standard till recently, will never be able to renounce this one thing: that nature announces itself in some way or other that is identifiable through calculation and that it remains orderable as a system of information. . . . It seems as though causality is shrinking into an announcing—an announcing challenged forth—of standing-reserves that must be guaranteed either simultaneously or in sequence.

97. Martin Heidegger, "Time and Being," in *Zur Sache des Denkens* (Tübingen: Max Niemeyer Verlag, 1969), p. 8. English translation: Martin Heidegger, *On Time and Being*, trans. Joan Stambaugh (New York: Harper & Row, 1972), p. 8.

98. Cf. Martin Heidegger, *Zur Sache des Denkens*, p. 40/*On Time and Being*, p. 37.

99. Alluding to the 33⅓ rpm LP, Pfullingen: Günther Neske Verlag, 1957. TN: The recorded text is now available on compact disc: Martin Heidegger, *Der Satz der Identität*, rec. 27 June, 1957, CD (Stuttgart: Verlag Günther Neske, 1997).

100. Martin Heidegger, *Zur Sache des Denkens*, p. 57/*On Time and Being*, p. 53.

101. "Letter on Humanism" in GA 9: 342/*Pathmarks*, p. 260.

102. The wish of the French seminar participants, to hear the German verb *bergen* in the French *berger*, is not supported by an etymological connection (*berger* stems from the Latin *berbicarius* [*berbix, brebis*, sheep] and thus literally means "the shepherd"). But indeed, *héberger* does come from the same root as the German *Herbergen* [inn, hostel, shelter].

103. Cf. Martin Heidegger, *Kant und das Problem der Metaphysik*, GA 3, ed. Friedrich-Wilhelm von Herrmann, 1991, §41, p. 229: "More original than the human is the finitude of Dasein in him." English translation: Martin Heidegger, *Kant and the Problem of Metaphysics*, 5th enlarged ed., trans. Richard Taft (Bloomington: Indiana University Press, 1997), p. 160.

104. Martin Heidegger, *Being and Time*, §§ 14–24.

105. Martin Heidegger, *Being and Time*, p. 352.

106. Martin Heidegger, "On the Essence of Ground," GA 9: 155, n. 55. English translation: *Pathmarks*, p. 370, n. 59.

107. Martin Heidegger, *Being and Time*, p. 1.

108. Edmund Husserl, *Logical Investigations*, Vol. 2, p. 775. TN: Investigation 6, section 2, chapter 6, § 40.

109. Edmund Husserl, *Logical Investigations*, Vol. 2, p. 775.

110. Simplicius, *On Aristotle's "Categories 7–8,"* trans. Barrie Fleet, ed. Richard Sorabji (Ithaca, N.Y.: Cornell University Press, 2000), p. 67. TN: The German text erroneously lists this passage as scolia to 66 b 45, it is actually a scholia to 8 b 25.

111. Cf. Jean Beaufret, *Dialogue avec Heidegger*, Vol. 3 (Paris: Minuit, 1974), p. 126.

112. TN: Immanuel Kant, *Critique of Pure Reason*, B xi, tm. Friedrich Hölderlin, "*Anmerkungen zur Antigonae*," pp. 265–272 in GSA 5, *Übersetzungen*, ed. Friedrich Beißner, 1952, p. 271. English translation: "Remarks on 'Antigone,'" pp. 109–116 in Friedrich Hölderlin, *Essays and Letters on Theory*, p. 114.

113. Martin Heidegger, *Zur Sache des Denkens*, pp. 81–90/*On Time and Being*, pp. 74–82.

114. Martin Heidegger, "The Origin of the Work of Art," in Martin Heidegger, *Holzwege*, GA 5, ed. Friedrich-Wilhelm von Herrmann, 1977, pp. 1–74. English translation in: Martin Heidegger, *Off the Beaten Track*, pp. 1–56. Martin Heidegger, "The Thing," in Martin Heidegger, *Vorträge und Aufsätze*, pp. 157–179. English translation in: Martin Heidegger, *Poetry, Language, Thought*, pp. 163–186.

115. TN: "We are precisely on a plane where there are only human beings."

116. GA 9: 334/*Pathmarks*, p. 254; tm: "We are precisely on a plane where principally there is being."

117. Karl Marx, *Die Frühschriften*, ed. Siefried Landshut (Stuttgart: Alfred Kröner Verlag, 1968). English translation in: Karl Marx, "Contribution to the Critique of Hegel's Philosophy of Law," trans. Martin Mulligan and Barbara Ruhemann, CW 3, p. 182.

118. See, for example, chapter 7, "The Crisis of Progress," in Robert Heiss's *Utopie und Revolution* (Munich: R. Piper & Co. Verlag, 1973).

119. Jacob Burckhardt, *Griechische Kulturgeschichte*, 4 Vols. (Basel, Switzerland: Benno Schwabe & Co., Verlag, 1956). Partial English translation in: Jacob Burckhardt, *The Greeks and Greek Civilization*, trans. Sheila Stern, ed. Oswyn Murray (London: HarperCollins, 1998).

120. TN: Karl Marx, "Contribution to the Critique of Hegel's Philosophy of Law," CW 3, p. 182.

121. TN: Karl Marx, "Contribution to the Critique of Hegel's Philosophy of Law," CW 3, p. 182.

122. Heidegger thinks of "nihilism" as "the fundamental movement of the history of the West . . . not only a phenomenon of the present age, nor even a product originally of the nineteenth century . . ." (GA 5: 201–202/*Off the Beaten Track*, pp. 163–164; cf. also "On the Question of Being" in GA 9: 385–426/*Pathmarks*, pp. 291–322; *Nietzsche*, vols. 1–2/ *Nietzsche*, vols. 1–4).

123. Martin Heidegger, *Zur Sache des Denkens*, p. 78/*On Time and Being*, p. 71.

124. TN: In both this sentence and the sentence before it, "domain of the inapparent" is a translation of *"Bereich des Unscheinbaren,"* which is what the text reads in the *Collected Edition* version of the seminars (see GA 15: 397). The single edition of the text reads here *"Bereich des Nichterscheinenden"* (Martin Heidegger, *Vier Seminare*, p. 135). The editor of the *Collected Edition* volume states that "discovered errors were corrected" in the reprinted text (GA 15: 442). We are indebted to Prof. Dr. Heinrich Hüni for this observation.

125. Martin Heidegger, *Being and Time*, p. 25.

126. Martin Heidegger, *"Wege zur Aussprache,"* GA 13: 15.

127. GA 13: 19.

128. GA 13: 19.

129. GA 13: 19.

130. Cf. Jean Wahl, *Existence humaine et transcendance* (Neuchâtel: L'Age d'Homme, 1944). In a French translation, pp. 134–135, Heidegger's letter of refusal, in which he objects to the erroneous conception of his thinking as existential philosophy, is reproduced.

131. GA 13: 18.

132. GA 13: 20.

133. Martin Heidegger, *"Lettre sur l'humanisme,"* traduite et présentée par Roger Munier (Paris: Aubier, 1964), p. 184.

134. Cf. Jean Beaufret, *Le poème de Parménide*, (Paris: PUF, 1955), p. viii.

135. TN: Martin Heidegger, *Was ist das—die Philosophie?* (Pfullingen: Verlag Günther Neske, 1956). English translation: Martin Heidegger, *What Is Philosophy?* trans. Jean T. Wilde and William Kluback (Albany: NCUP, 1958).

136. At that time, Char had already read writings of Heidegger; cf. René Char,

Recherche de la base et du sommet, (Paris: Gallimard, 1971), p. 149. The *Impressions anciennes,* begun in 1950, are dedicated to Heidegger.

137. *Questions IV,* p. 196.

138. Martin Heidegger and Eugen Fink, *Heraklit* (Frankfurt am Main: Vittorio Klostermann, 1970). English translation: Martin Heidegger and Eugen Fink, *Heraclitus Seminar,* trans. Charles H. Siebert (Evanston, Ill.: Northwestern University Press, 1993).

139. Martin Heidegger, *Erläuterungen zu Hölderlins Dichtung,* 2d expanded ed., Friedrich-Wilhelm von Herrmann, GA 4, 1996, pp. 156-181. English translation: Martin Heidegger, *Elucidations of Hölderlin's Poetry* (Amherst, N.Y.: Humanity Books, 2000), 175-207.

140. *"Réponses interrogatives à une question de Martin Heidegger,"* in: René Char, *Recherche de la base et du sommet,* pp. 133-136. On the conversation with Char cf. François Vezin, *"Heidegger parle en France,"* in *Nouvelle Revue Française,* Nr. 284 (Paris: Août, 1976), pp. 85-86.

141. Contribution without title to: *Aujourd'hui Rimbaud . . .* Enquête de Roger Munier, No. 160 (Paris: Minard, 1976), pp. 13-17. (German text and French translation). Reprinted as *"Rimbaud vivant"* in GA 13: 225-227.

142. Martin Heidegger, *Erläuterungen zu Hölderlins Dichtung,* GA 4: 182-192/ *Elucidations of Hölderlin's Poetry,* pp. 209-219.

143. TN: See *Pathmarks,* pp. 231-238 and 277-290.

144. The sentence which here expands the question in comparison with the text on p. 78, reads in translation: "Does it belong in that open region (*Gegnet* [citation from *Gelassenheit*]), in which the human freely unfolds his essence?"

145. In French translation as a prefatory note to Munier's translation of "What is Metaphysics?" which appeared in *Le Nouveau Commerce,* Cahier 14 (Paris: José Corti, 1969), pp. 57-59.

146. TN: A mountain range in the northeast of France.

147. The naming of Cézanne is no aesthetic Arabesque. Before the 1958 lecture in Aix, Heidegger had said that his own path of thought responded in its way to the artistic path of Cézanne. Cf. Jean Beaufret, *Dialogue avec Heidegger.* Vol. 3. (Paris: Minuit, 1974), pp. 155-156.

The highpoint of an excursion to Aix-en-Provence during the seminar of 1968 was the visit to Cézanne's studio in Chemin des Lauves, mentioned by Heidegger in "Cézanne" from the poem cycle *"Gedachtes." L'Herne,* special number dedicated to René Char. Ed. Dominique Fourcade (Paris: l'Herne, 1971), p. 183. TN: *"Gedachtes"* in GA 13: 221-224; "Cézanne," GA 13: 223.

148. TN: Friedrich Hölderlin, *"Vom Abgrund nemlich. . . ,"* GSA 2.1: 250-251. English translation in: Friedrich Hölderlin, *Hymns and Fragments,* 198-201. The reference to Provence reads:

> Berries, like coral,
> Hang from shrubs over wooden pipes
> Out of which
> First from grain, now from flowers, fortified song
> As new culture from the city, where nostrils
> Nearly ache with the rising
> Scent of lemon and oil from Provence, such gratitude
> Have the lands of Gascogne
> Granted me. [21-31]

149. Martin Heidegger, *Acheminement vers la parole* (Paris: Gallimard, 1976), pp. 7–8 — Albert Camus had lived in Lourmarin and is buried there. TN: A translation:

> Words from René Char, who attested for us the
> nearness of poetry and thinking:
>
> > In my country, the tender proofs
> > of spring and the shabby birds
> > are preferable to distant goals.
> >
> > . . . .
> >
> > In my country, one thanks.
> >
> > *
> >
> > With the one we love we have
> > ceased to speak, and this is not silence.
> > Eternity in Lourmarin Albert Camus.
> >
> > *
> >
> > The word raises more earth
> > than the undertaker is able to.
> >
> > *
>
> Is beloved Provence the secretive
> invisible bridge from the early thinking
> of Parmenides to the poetry of Hölderlin?
> M.H.

150. Martin Heidegger, *"Aus der Erfahrung des Denkens,"* GA 13: 82. English translation in: Martin Heidegger, *Poetry, Language, Thought,* p. 10, tm.

151. Martin Heidegger,"The End of Philosophy and the Task of Thinking," in Martin Heidegger, *Zur Sache des Denkens,* pp. 78–80/*On Time and Being,* pp. 70–73.

152. Brackets appear in the manuscript.

153. J. W. von Goethe, "Introduction to the *Propyläen* (1798)," pp. 3–16 in J. W. von Goethe, *Goethe on Art,* ed. and trans. John Gage (Berkeley: University of California Press, 1980), p. 4, tm. TN: the quotation continues, "that we do not long remain quiet observers, but begin to reflect."

154. TN: Martin Heidegger, *Was Heißt Denken?* 4th ed. (Tübingen: Max Niemeyer Verlag, 1984), p. 34. English translation: Martin Heidegger, *What Is Called Thinking?* trans. J. Glenn Gray (New York: Harper & Row, 1968), p. 89. The abbreviated form stands in the manuscript. Karl Rosenkranz, *Georg Wilhelm Friedrich Hegels Leben beschrieben durch Karl Rosenkranz: Supplement zu Hegels Werken* (Berlin: Duncker und Humblot, 1844), p. 552.

155. TN: A collection of Hegel's notes dating from 1803–1806. See Rosenkranz, 198–201. For a partial English translation, see reference in note 39, above.

156. Martin Heidegger, GA 5: 138. English translation in: Martin Heidegger, *Off the Beaten Track,* p. 104.

157. TN: G. W. F. Hegel, "Hegel to Schelling," 30 August, 1795, in G. W. F. Hegel, *Hegel: The Letters,* trans. Clark Butler and Christiane Seiler, ed. Clark Butler (Bloomington: Indiana University Press, 1984), p. 43.

158. Martin Heidegger, *Was Heißt Denken?* p. 34/*What Is Called Thinking?* p. 90.

Glossary: German-English

German	English
abbauen	to dismantle
Abgekommensein, das	departure
abkehren	to turn away from
abkommen	to depart
abwenden	to turn away from
angehen	to encounter
ankündigende Vorzeichen, das	the heralding portent
Anschauung, die	intuition
Anwesen machen	to make present
anwesen	to presence; presencing
Anwesen, das	presencing; to presence
anwesend	presencing
Anwesende, das	what presences
Anwesenheit, die	presence
Anwesen-lassen, das	to let come to presence
Anwesung, die	presenting
Aufeinanderfolge, die	succession
Aufenthalt, der	residence
aufhalten	to reside
Aufhebung, die	sublation
Ausdrück, der	expression
Auseinanderfolge, die	development
Aussage, die	proposition
aussagen	to make a proposition
Bedeutung, die	significance, signification
Bedrängnis, die	pressure
Bedrängung, die	rush
Bedurfnis, das	need
Behutsamkeit, die	sheltering
Besinnung, die	meditation
Bestand, der	standing reserve
Beständbarkeit, die	standing-reservedness
Bestellbarkeit, die	orderability
bewahren	to preserve
Bewahren, das	preserve, preserving
Bewegtheit, die	movedness
bewirtschaft	economic
Bewußtlose, der	non-conscious
Bewußtsein, das	consciousness
Bodenbewirtschaftung, die	agriculture
durchstimmen	to thoroughly attune
Einkehr, die	entry
Entbergung, die	disclosure
Entgegensetzung, die	opposition
entzweien	to diverge

Entzweiung, die	dichotomy
Ent-zweiung, die	scission
erblicken	to glimpse; gaze
Ereignis, das	enowning
festgeworden	rigid
Festmachen, das	stabilization
fixierte	fixed
Fixierung, die	fixity, fixing
Freie, das	free dimension
Gegensatz, der	opposite
Gegenüberstehen, das	polarity
Gelassenheit, die	releasement
Geschick, das	destiny
geschicklich	destinal
Ge-stell, das	positionality
gewahren	to safeguard
heimisch zu werden	to become at home
Herausforderung, die	challenge, challenging forth
Herkunft, die	provenance
hüten	to protect
Inständigkeit, die	instancy
kategoriale Anschauung, die	categorial intuition
Kehre, die	the turn
Kontrast, der	contrast
Körper, der	body
lassen das Anwesen	to let the presencing
lassen	letting, to let; to allow
Leib, der	lived-body
leibhaftig	bodily
Leibhaftigkeit, die	corporeality
Macht der Vereinigung, die	power of conjoining
Miteinanderzusammengehörigkeit, die	co-belonging
Negation, die	negation
Nicht, das	the nothing
nichten	to negate
nichtend	nihilating
Nichtigkeit, die	nothingness
Obhut, die	shelter
Ort, der	place
Örtlichkeit, die	locality
Ortschaft, die	location
Putz, der	embellishment
Riß, der	rift
Sache, die	matter
Sachverhalt, der	state of affairs
Satz, der	statement
Schicken, das	sending
Schickung, die	sending
Schmuck, der	decoration

Sein-lassen, das	letting-be
Seinsgeschick, das	destiny of being
Setzen, das	positing, to posit
Seyn, das	be-ing
sich umkehren	to turn upside down
Sichentzweienden, die	the diverging-ones
Sinn, der	meaning
sinnliche Anschauung, die	sensuous intuition
sinnliche Gegebene, das	sense data
sinnliche	sensuous
Sinnlichkeit, die	sensibility
Übermaß, das	excess
Überschuss, der	surplus
Umkehr, die	reversal, reverse, turn around
Unbewußte, das	the unconscious
Unentzweiteste, das	most non-dichotomous
Unscheinbare, das	inapparent
Verbrauch, der	consumption
verbraucht	consumed
Vereinigung, die	conjoining
Verfall, der	fall
verfügbar	disposable
Verfügbarkeit, die	disposability
Vergegenwärtigung, die	making present
verneinen	to deny
Verstand, der	understanding
Verwahrung, die	safe keeping
wahren	to guard
währen	to last
Wanderung, die	sojourn
Weite, die	expanse
Weltanschauung, die	world-intuition
widersprechende	contradictory
Widerspruch, der	contradiction
Widerwendigen, die	contraries
zer-reissen	to tear apart
Zer-rissene, das	what is torn apart
Zerrissenheit, die	the tearing
Zier, die	adornment
Zugeschickte, das	that which is destined
zukehren	to turn to, turn toward
zurückkehren	to turn back
zurückwenden	to turn back
zusammengehören	to belong together
Zusammengehörigkeit, die	belonging together
zuschicken	to destine
zusprechen	to address
zuwenden	to turn to, turn toward
Zwang, der	constraint

Glossary: English-German

to address	zusprechen
adornment	Zier, die
agriculture	Bodenbewirtschaftung, die
to become at home	heimisch zu werden
be-ing	Seyn, das
to belong together	zusammengehören
belonging together	Zusammengehörigkeit, die
bodily	leibhaftig
body	Körper, der
categorial intuition	kategoriale Anschauung, die
challenge, challenging forth	Herausforderung, die
co-belonging	Miteinanderzusammengehörigkeit, die
conjoining	Vereinigung, die
consciousness	Bewußtsein, das
constraint	Zwang, der
consumed	verbraucht
consumption	Verbrauch, der
contradiction	Widerspruch, der
contradictory	widersprechende
contraries	Widerwendigen, die
contrast	Kontrast, der
corporeality	Leibhaftigkeit, die
decoration	Schmuck, der
to deny	verneinen
to depart	abkommen
departure	Abgekommensein, das
destinal	geschicklich
to destine	zuschicken
that which is destined	Zugeschickte, das
destiny of being	Seinsgeschick, das
destiny	Geschick, das
development	Auseinanderfolge, die
dichotomy	Entzweiung, die
disclosure	Entbergung, die
to dismantle	abbauen
disposability	Verfügbarkeit, die
disposable	verfügbar
to diverge	entzweien
the diverging-ones	Sichentzweienden, die
economic	bewirtschaft
embellishment	Putz, der
to encounter	angehen
enowning	Ereignis, das
entry	Einkehr, die
excess	Übermaß, das
expanse	Weite, die

expression	Ausdrück, der
fall	Verfall, der
fixed	fixierte
fixity, fixing	Fixierung, die
free dimension	Freie, das
to glimpse; gaze	erblicken
to guard	wahren
the heralding portent	ankündigende Vorzeichnen, das
inapparent	Unscheinbare, das
instancy	Inständigkeit, die
intuition	Anschauung, die
to last	währen
to let come to presence	Anwesen-lassen, das
to let the presencing	lassen das Anwesen
letting, to let; to allow	lassen
letting-be	Sein-lassen, das
lived-body	Leib, der
locality	Örtlichkeit, die
location	Ortschaft, die
to make a proposition	aussagen
to make present	Anwesen machen
making present	Vergegenwärtigung, die
matter	Sache, die
meaning	Sinn, der
meditation	Besinnung, die
most non-dichotomous	Unentzweiteste, das
movedness	Bewegtheit, die
need	Bedurfnis, das
to negate	nichten
negation	Negation, die
nihilating	nichtend
non-conscious	Bewußtlose, der
the nothing	Nicht, das
nothingness	Nichtigkeit, die
opposite	Gegensatz, der
opposition	Entgegensetzung, die
orderability	Bestellbarkeit, die
place	Ort, der
polarity	Gegenüberstehen, das
positing, to posit	Setzen, das
positionality	Ge-stell, das
power of conjoining	Macht der Vereinigung, die
presence	Anwesenheit, die
to presence; presencing	anwesen
what presences	Anwesende, das
presencing	anwesend
presencing; to presence	Anwesen, das
presenting	Anwesung, die

to preserve	bewahren
preserve, preserving	Bewahren, das
pressure	Bedrängnis, die
proposition	Aussage, die
to protect	hüten
provenance	Herkunft, die
releasement	Gelassenheit, die
to reside	aufhalten
residence	Aufenthalt, der
reversal, reverse, turn around	Umkehr, die
rift	Riß, der
rigid	festgeworden
rush	Bedrängung, die
safe keeping	Verwahrung, die
to safeguard	gewahren
scission	Ent-zweiung, die
sending	Schicken, das
sending	Schickung, die
sense data	sinnliche Gegebene, das
sensibility	Sinnlichkeit, die
sensuous intuition	sinnliche Anschauung, die
sensuous	sinnliche
shelter	Obhut, die
sheltering	Behutsamkeit, die
significance, signification	Bedeutung, die
sojourn	Wanderung, die
stabilization	Festmachen, das
standing reserve	Bestand, der
standing-reservedness	Beständbarkeit, die
state of affairs	Sachverhalt, der
statement	Satz, der
sublation	Aufhebung, die
succession	Aufeinanderfolge, die
surplus	Überschuss, der
to tear apart	zer-reissen
the tearing	Zerrissenheit, die
to thoroughly attune	durchstimmen
what is torn apart	Zer-rissene, das
the turn	Kehre, die
to turn away from	abkehren
to turn away from	abwenden
to turn back	zurückkehren
to turn back	zurückwenden
to turn to, turn toward	zukehren
to turn to, turn toward	zuwenden
to turn upside down	sich umkehren
the unconscious	Unbewußte, das
understanding	Verstand, der
world-intuition	Weltanschauung, die